STICKNEY-FOREST VIEW LIBRARY DISTRICT

3 1803 00125 28

S0-ARM-091

STICKNEY FOREST VIEW LIBRARY
6800 W. 43RD STREET
STICKNEY, IL 60402

DEMCO

DWI, DUI AND THE LAW

by
Margaret C. Jasper

Oceana's Legal Almanac Series:
Law for the Layperson

2004
Oceana Publications, Inc.
Dobbs Ferry, New York

Information contained in this work has been obtained by Oceana Publications from sources believed to be reliable. However, neither the Publisher nor its authors guarantee the accuracy or completeness of any information published herein, and neither Oceana nor its authors shall be responsible for any errors, omissions or damages arising from the use of this information. This work is published with the understanding that Oceana and its authors are supplying information, but are not attempting to render legal or other professional services. If such services are required, the assistance of an appropriate professional should be sought.

You may order this or any Oceana publication by visiting Oceana's website at http://www.oceanalaw.com

Library of Congress Control Number: 2004105891

ISBN 0-379-11383-X

Oceana's Legal Almanac Series: Law for the Layperson

ISSN 1075-7376

©2004 by Oceana Publications, Inc.

All rights reserved. No part of this publication may be reproduced or transmitted in any form or by any means, electronic or mechanical, including photocopy, recording, xerography, or any information storage and retrieval system, without permission in writing from the publisher.

Manufactured in the United States of America on acid-free paper.

To My Husband Chris

Your love and support
are my motivation and inspiration

-and-

In memory of my son, Jimmy

Table of Contents

CHAPTER 2:
ELEMENTS OF THE DRUNK DRIVING OFFENSE

CHAPTER 3:
BAC DETECTION METHODS

CHAPTER 4:
UNDERAGE DRINKING AND DRIVING

CHAPTER 5:
DETERRENCE AND ENFORCEMENT MEASURES

CHAPTER 6:
FEDERAL LEGISLATION PROGRAMS

CHAPTER 7:
VICTIMS RIGHTS

APPENDICES

ABOUT THE AUTHOR

MARGARET C. JASPER is an attorney engaged in the general practice of law in South Salem, New York, concentrating in the areas of personal injury and entertainment law. Ms. Jasper holds a Juris Doctor degree from Pace University School of Law, White Plains, New York, is a member of the New York and Connecticut bars, and is certified to practice before the United States District Courts for the Southern and Eastern Districts of New York, the United States Court of Appeals for the Second Circuit, and the United States Supreme Court.

Ms. Jasper has been appointed to the panel of arbitrators of the American Arbitration Association and the law guardian panel for the Family Court of the State of New York, is a member of the Association of Trial Lawyers of America, and is a New York State licensed real estate broker and member of the Westchester County Board of Realtors, operating as Jasper Real Estate, in South Salem, New York. She maintains a website at http://www.JasperLawOffice.com.

Ms. Jasper is the author and general editor of the following legal almanacs: AIDS Law; The Americans with Disabilities Act; Animal Rights Law; The Law of Attachment and Garnishment; Bankruptcy Law for the Individual Debtor; Individual Bankruptcy and Restructuring; Banks and their Customers; Buying and Selling Your Home; The Law of Buying and Selling; The Law of Capital Punishment; The Law of Child Custody; Commercial Law; Consumer Rights Law; The Law of Contracts; Copyright Law; Credit Cards and the Law; The Law of Debt Collection; Dictionary of Selected Legal Terms; The Law of Dispute Resolution; The Law of Drunk Driving; DWI, DUI and the Law; Education Law; Elder Law; Employee Rights in the Workplace; Employment Discrimination Under Title VII; Environmental Law; Estate Planning; Everyday Legal Forms; Executors and Personal Representatives: Rights and Responsibilities; Harassment in the Workplace; Health Care and Your Rights. Home Mortgage Law Primer; Hospital Liability

Law; Identity Theft and How To Protect Yourself; Insurance Law; The Law of Immigration; International Adoption; Juvenile Justice and Children's Law; Labor Law; Landlord-Tenant Law; The Law of Libel and Slander; Living Together: Practical Legal Issues; Marriage and Divorce; The Law of Medical Malpractice; Motor Vehicle Law; The Law of No-Fault Insurance; Nursing Home Negligence; The Law of Obscenity and Pornography; Patent Law; The Law of Personal Injury; Privacy and the Internet: Your Rights and Expectations Under the Law; Probate Law; The Law of Product Liability; Real Estate Law for the Homeowner and Broker; Religion and the Law; The Right to Die; Law for the Small Business Owner; Social Security Law; Special Education Law; The Law of Speech and the First Amendment; Teenagers and Substance Abuse; Trademark Law; Victim's Rights Law; The Law of Violence Against Women; Welfare: Your Rights and the Law; What if it Happened to You: Violent Crimes and Victims' Rights; What if the Product Doesn't Work: Warranties & Guarantees; Workers' Compensation Law; and Your Child's Legal Rights: An Overview.

INTRODUCTION

Laws designed to prevent drunk driving have been on the books in all jurisdictions for many years, some dating back to the time the automobile first made its appearance. Due in large part to strong enforcement initiatives and public awareness campaigns seeking to strengthen these laws, the incidence of alcohol-impaired driving has been reduced in recent years. Nevertheless, drinking and driving is still a major safety problem.

A number of national organizations have emerged to join in the effort to stop drunk driving, including Mothers Against Drunk Driving (MADD); Students Against Drunk Driving (SADD); and the National Commission Against Drunk Driving (NCADD). These national organizations have been founded to increase public awareness of the dangers of drunk driving. They have successfully lobbied state legislatures to stiffen penalties to punish and deter drunk driving in an effort to prevent a second or subsequent offense.

This almanac sets forth a general discussion of the law as it applies to drunk driving, including the elements of the drunk driving offense and the scope of the problem, blood alcohol concentration levels and testing, victims' rights, and the penalties one may be subjected to if convicted of drunk driving. The problem of underage drinking and legislation addressing reduced alcohol impairment levels applicable to young drivers is also set forth in this almanac. The federal legislative programs designed to reduce drunk driving are also explored.

Because the law differs among jurisdictions, the reader is advised to check the law of his or her jurisdiction for specific information.

The Appendix provides relevant laws and other pertinent information and data. The drunk driving law as contained in the Uniform Vehicle Code is also set forth in the Appendix and explored herein. The Glossary contains definitions of many of the terms used throughout the almanac.

CHAPTER 1:
STATISTICAL OVERVIEW

SCOPE OF THE PROBLEM

Drinking and driving is the most frequently committed violent crime in America. The statistics are alarming. According to the National Highway Traffic Safety Administration (NHTSA), somebody dies in an alcohol-related crash every thirty minutes and someone is injured every two minutes. It is estimated that about two in every five Americans will be involved in an alcohol-related crash at some time in their lives.

According to the NHTSA, almost 1.4 million people have died in traffic crashes in the United States since 1966. During the late 1960's and early 1970's, more than 50,000 people lost their lives each year on the nation's public roads and highways, and more than half of the drivers killed had been drinking.

Nevertheless, because traffic safety has improved since that time, in large part due to legislation which created the NHTSA in 1966, the annual death rate has declined considerably, to about 40,000, even though the number of drivers, vehicles and miles driven have all greatly increased. Using miles traveled as a measuring stick, the likelihood of being killed in a traffic accident in 1966 was more than three times what it is today.

Despite these dramatic improvements in traffic safety, an average of more than 115 people still die each day from motor vehicle accidents in the United States, and it is estimated that 41 percent of the drivers who die in crashes have been drinking.

Drinking and driving-related injuries and fatalities have become so prevalent that concerted efforts to combat the problem have increased significantly. Many organizations have emerged to increase public awareness, and have successfully lobbied for the passage and enforcement of more stringent drunk driving laws. In fact, according to the

NHTSA, more than 2,300 anti-drunk driving laws have been passed since 1980.

A directory of NHTSA regional offices is set forth at Appendix 1.

RECENT STATISTICS

Despite efforts to deter drunk driving, alcohol-related traffic fatalities still pose a grave and dangerous problem. In 2002, traffic fatalities in alcohol-related crashes rose slightly—from 17,400 in 2001 to 17,419 in 2002. The 17,419 alcohol-related fatalities in 2002 represent 41 percent of total traffic fatalities for the year, and an average of one alcohol-related fatality every 30 minutes.

Nationwide, in 2002, alcohol was present in 25 percent of the drivers involved in fatal crashes, and of this total, 21 percent had a BAC level of 0.08% or greater. In addition, an estimated 258,000 persons were injured in crashes where police reported that alcohol was present—an average of one person injured every 2 minutes.

In 2002, 35 percent of all traffic fatalities occurred in crashes in which at least one driver or nonoccupant had a BAC of 0.08 or greater. Sixty-eight percent of the 15,019 people killed in such crashes were themselves intoxicated. The remaining 32 percent were passengers, nonintoxicated drivers, or nonintoxicated nonoccupants.

A table depicting the types of fatalities in crashes involving at least one intoxicated driver or nonoccupant in 2002 is set forth at Appendix 2.

BAC Level

In 2002, 12,344 of the 14,662 drivers (84%) who had been drinking with a BAC level of 0.01 or higher, and who were involved in fatal crashes, had a BAC level at or above the intoxication level of 0.08.

A table depicting the total number of traffic fatalities in 2002, by state and BAC level, is set forth at Appendix 3.

Time of Day

A greater proportion of nighttime drivers involved in fatal crashes tend to have alcohol in their system as compared to daytime drivers involved in fatal crashes. In fact, the rate of alcohol involvement in fatal crashes is more than 3 times as high at night as during the day (63% vs. 19%). For all crashes, the alcohol involvement rate is 5 times as high at night (15% vs. 3%). Among passenger vehicle drivers fatally injured between 9 pm and 6 am in 2002, 59 percent had BACs at or above 0.08 percent, compared with 18 percent during other hours.

A table depicting the number of driver fatalities in 2002, by time of day and BAC level, is set forth at Appendix 4.

Day of the Week

A greater proportion of drivers involved in fatal crashes on the weekend tend to have alcohol in their system as compared to drivers involved in fatal crashes on weekdays. In 2002, 31 percent of all fatal crashes during the week were alcohol-related, compared to 54 percent on weekends. Forty-five percent of fatally injured drivers on weekends in 2002 had BACs at or above 0.08 percent. At other times the proportion was 25 percent. For all crashes, the alcohol involvement rate was 4 percent during the week and 11 percent during the weekend.

A table depicting the number of driver fatalities in 2002, by day of week and BAC level, is set forth at Appendix 5.

Age

From 1992 to 2002, intoxication rates (i.e., BAC of 0.08 or greater) decreased for drivers of all age groups involved in fatal crashes, except for the group of drivers 45 to 64 years old, which had the same rates in 1992 and 2002. Drivers over 64 years old experienced the largest decrease in intoxication rates (29%), followed by drivers 25 to 34 years old (20%). The highest intoxication rates in fatal crashes in 2002 were recorded for drivers 21-24 years old (33%), followed by ages 25-34 (28%), and 35-44 (26%).

A table depicting the number of drivers involved in fatal crashes in 2002, by age and BAC level, is set forth at Appendix 6.

Gender

Statistics show that male drivers involved in fatal crashes are twice as likely to have consumed alcohol as compared to female drivers. Alcohol involvement in fatal crashes is highest for men who are 21-40 years old. In 2001, the alcohol involvement among male drivers was 29 percent while that for female drivers was 16 percent. In 2002, there were 42,135 male drivers involved in fatal crashes, 25% of whom had a BAC level at or exceeding 0.08%. There were also 14,911 female drivers involved in fatal crashes, 12% of whom had a BAC level at or exceeding 0.08%.

A table depicting the number of drivers involved in fatal crashes in 2001, by gender and BAC level, is set forth at Appendix 7.

Type of Vehicle

Intoxication rates for drivers in fatal crashes in 2002 were highest for motorcycle operators (31%), and lowest for drivers of large trucks (2%).

The intoxication rate for drivers of light trucks (23%) was higher than that for passenger car drivers (22%).

A table depicting the number of drivers involved in fatal crashes in 2002, by vehicle type and BAC level, is set forth at Appendix 8.

Safety Belts

A greater proportion of drivers who did not use safety belts and who were involved in fatal crashes had alcohol in their system as compared to drivers involved in fatal crashes who did wear safety belts. In 2002, safety belts were used by only 23 percent of the fatally injured intoxicated drivers, i.e., those with a BAC level of 0.08 or greater, compared to 36 percent of fatally injured impaired drivers, i.e., those with a BAC level between 0.01 and 0.07, and 53 percent of fatally injured sober drivers.

A table depicting the number of drivers involved in fatal crashes in 2001, by safety belt use and BAC level, is set forth at Appendix 9.

Type of Injury

A fatally injured driver is about twice as likely to have consumed alcohol as compared to a driver who survived the crash. Fatally injured drivers are tested for alcohol by the medical examiner. In 2001, the proportion of all alcohol-related fatally injured drivers was about twice that of all drivers who survived a fatal crash. Thus, it is reasonable to infer that drivers who survive fatal crashes are intoxicated much less frequently than fatally injured drivers.

A table depicting the number of drivers involved in fatal crashes in 2001, by injury severity and BAC level, is set forth at Appendix 10.

Child Victims

The NHTSA estimates that one out of every 280 babies born today will die in an automobile accident with an intoxicated driver. In 2002, 22% of the 2,197 traffic fatalities among children ages 0 to 14 years involved alcohol. Almost two-thirds of children under 15 who died in alcohol-related crashes between 1985 and 1996 were riding with the drinking driver.

Prior Convictions

According to the NHTSA, in fatal crashes, drivers with prior DWI convictions are more than three times as likely to be intoxicated as compared to those that do not have any prior DWI convictions. Drivers with one or more prior DWI convictions were more than twice as likely to be intoxicated when involved in a fatal crash. In 2001, among drivers with no prior DWI convictions, 20 percent were intoxicated as compared to 62 percent of those drivers who had one or more prior DWI convictions.

A table depicting the extent of intoxication among drivers involved in fatal crashes from 1997 to 2001, by prior convictions of the driver, is set forth at Appendix 11.

Fatally injured drivers with BAC levels of 0.08 or greater were 5 times as likely to have a prior conviction for driving while intoxicated compared to fatally injured sober drivers.

A table depicting the previous driving records of drivers killed in traffic crashes in 2002, by BAC level, is set forth at Appendix 12.

Pedestrian Traffic Accidents

More than one-third (36%) of all pedestrians 16 years of age or older killed in traffic crashes in 2002 were intoxicated. By age group, the percentages ranged from a low of 10 percent for pedestrians 65 and over to a high of 53 percent for those 35 to 44 years old.

The driver, pedestrian, or both were intoxicated in 41 percent of all fatal pedestrian crashes in 2002. In these crashes, the intoxication rate for pedestrians (34%) was nearly triple the rate for drivers (13%). Both the pedestrian and the driver were intoxicated in 5 percent of the crashes that resulted in a pedestrian fatality.

A table depicting the number of pedestrians killed in fatal crashes in 2002, by age and BAC level, is set forth at Appendix 13.

Type of Crash

According to the NHTSA, in fatal crashes, drivers in single vehicle crashes are about three times as likely to be intoxicated as drivers who are involved in multiple vehicle crashes.

A table depicting the number of drivers killed in fatal crashes in 2002, by type of crash and BAC level, is set forth at Appendix 14.

DRUG USE AND DRIVING

There is much less information concerning the role of drugs in motor vehicle accidents as compared to alcohol, although it is estimated that drugs other than alcohol—e.g., marijuana and cocaine—have been identified as factors in 18% of motor vehicle driver deaths. Many drug-impaired drivers are never detected or, when detected, are arrested as alcohol-impaired only. Drug users often drink alcohol to disguise their use of drugs. If involved in crashes, drug users are not chemically tested for drugs other than alcohol. When information is obtained on a driver's drug use, it typically comes from hospital tests performed on those who are killed in crashes, or hospitalized with crash injuries.

It has been established that many legal and illegal drugs can impair driving ability, even in moderate concentrations, and may increase the risk of accidents. However, there is presently insufficient scientific evidence concerning the effect of drugs, other than alcohol, on driving. According to a 1988 NHTSA report, the drugs with the most potential to be serious highway safety hazards are tranquilizers, sedatives and hypnotics, e.g. barbiturates. However, it is difficult to ascertain what contribution drugs have made in motor vehicle crashes. Conservative estimates suggest that thousands die and tens of thousands are injured annually as a result of drug-impaired driving.

A 1992 study revealed that alcohol was found in fifty-two percent of 1,882 fatally injured drivers. Forty-three percent had blood alcohol concentrations of 0.10 percent or more. Only six percent had drugs without alcohol, and researchers found no evidence that drivers with drugs but no alcohol are more likely to be responsible for their crashes, compared with drug-free drivers. The researchers did find that drugs were related to crash responsibility when combined with alcohol, or when two or more drugs were found.

Nevertheless, the use of stimulants by tractor-trailer drivers has become a noteworthy problem. A National Transportation Safety Board (NTSB) investigation of fatal truck crashes found that stimulants were the most frequently identified drug class among fatally injured drivers, and were present in approximately 15 percent of those drivers.

Studies have been undertaken to assess the effect of stimulants. It has been found that occasional use of stimulants may, in the short term, enhance the performance of some tasks by increasing alertness. However, some tractor-trailer drivers may use these drugs to continue on the road for prolonged periods. Use of stimulants for this purpose is probably frequent and sustained, not occasional, and thus is potentially dangerous.

COSTS

According to the NHTSA, automobile crashes claim about 42,000 lives each year in the United States. The associated costs to society are overwhelming: economic costs are approximately $150 billion, and include medical care and emergency expenses ($19 billion); lost productivity ($42 billion); property damage ($52 billion); and miscellaneous crash-related costs ($37 billion). Approximately thirty percent of these automobile accidents are alcohol-related, accounting for $45 billion in associated costs each year. This figure does not include pain and suffering, and lost quality of life, which significantly raise that figure.

The cost for each injured survivor of an alcohol-related crash averaged $67,000, including $6,000 in health care costs and $13,000 in lost productivity. In addition, over 25 percent of the first year of medical costs for persons hospitalized as a result of an automobile crash are paid by tax dollars, about two-thirds through Medicaid and one-third through Medicare.

ARREST RATE

According to the FBI, in 2001, more than 1.4 million drivers were arrested for driving under the influence of alcohol or narcotics, which accounts for slightly more than 1 percent of the 120 million self-reported episodes of alcohol–impaired driving among U.S. adults each year. This is an arrest rate of 1 for every 137 licensed drivers in the United States

PREVENTION INITIATIVES

A number of measures have been suggested, some of which have been implemented, in an attempt to prevent injuries and deaths caused by drunk driving, including:

1. Immediate suspension of driver's licenses of DWI offenders.

2. Lowering the permissible BAC level to 0.08% (some groups have suggested the BAC level should be further reduced to 0.05%).

3. Zero tolerance laws for drivers younger than 21 years old.

4. Sobriety checkpoints.

5. Community-based approaches to alcohol control and DUI prevention.

6. Mandatory substance abuse assessment and treatment for DWI offenders.

7. Raising state and federal alcohol excise taxes

8. Implementing compulsory blood alcohol testing when traffic crashes result in injury.

CHAPTER 2:
ELEMENTS OF THE DRUNK DRIVING OFFENSE

IN GENERAL

All jurisdictions have drunk driving statutes. This chapter provides an overview of the basic elements of drunk driving common to most state statutes. Although all of the statutes contain similar provisions, the broad terms used to describe the elements of the offense of drunk driving have subjected them to differing judicial interpretations. Thus, the reader is advised to check both the statute and case law of his or her jurisdiction when researching a particular issue.

COMMON MISCONCEPTIONS ABOUT ALCOHOL IMPAIRMENT

Alcohol impairment is a known contributor to motor vehicle accidents. It is a misconception, however, that one must be "drunk" in order to be a dangerous driver. Many alcohol-impaired drivers do not appear visibly drunk. Studies have indicated that even small amounts of alcohol can impair driving skills.

Another common misbelief is that the likelihood of impairment is contingent on the type of drink. Some mistakenly believe that beer, for instance, is less likely to cause impairment compared to hard liquor. However, impairment is not determined by the type of drink. It is measured by the amount of alcohol ingested over a specific period of time. In fact, beer is the most common drink consumed by people stopped for alcohol-impaired driving or involved in alcohol-related crashes.

Many believe that they have had enough time to "sober up" between the time they drink and the time they drive, and are unaware of how much time is actually needed for one's body to metabolize alcohol. Studies indicate that most people need at least one hour to metabolize one drink.

USE OF THE VEHICLE

The statutory construction used to describe the use of the vehicle in the crime of drunk driving differs among jurisdictions, although all jurisdictions include either the term "driving" or "operating" a motor vehicle as an essential element of the crime of drunk driving. For example, West Virginia specifies "drives" as the use of the vehicle. (W. Va. Code §17C-5-2), while Connecticut describes the necessary use of the vehicle as to "operate." (Conn. Gen. Stat. An. §14-227a). Mississippi uses both terms, describing the necessary use as "to drive or otherwise operate." (Miss. Code An. §63-11-30).

The term "driving" has been interpreted in the most narrowest sense, and generally requires the vehicle to be in motion. The term "operating" is more broad, and has been interpreted to include starting the engine or manipulating the mechanical or electrical devices of a standing vehicle.

Section 11-902 of the Uniform Vehicle Code, from which many jurisdictions have adopted language in full or in part for their own drunk driving statutes, describes the requisite act as being in "actual physical control," in conjunction with the term "driving":

> (a) A person shall not drive or be in *actual physical control* of any vehicle while (1) the alcohol concentration in such person's blood or breath is 0.08 or more. . .

For example, Idaho describes the use of vehicle element as to "drive or be in actual physical control." (Idaho Code §18-8004). Minnesota's statute includes all of the above, describing the necessary use as to "drive, operate, or be in physical control." (Minn. Stat. An. §169.121).

This statutory description is more inclusive than either "driving" or "operating." Actual physical control generally does not require the vehicle to be moving. For example, the Illinois Court of Appeals has applied this definition to an individual who is seated behind the steering wheel with the ignition key and physically capable of starting the engine and moving the vehicle.

Selected provisions of the Uniform Vehicle Code related to drunk driving are set forth at Appendix 15.

EVIDENCE OF DRIVING, OPERATING OR ACTUAL PHYSICAL CONTROL

Oftentimes, there is no direct evidence that an individual was driving, operating, or in control of a vehicle. For example, following a one-car accident, there are generally no witnesses, and the driver has likely exited the car. Although the driver may admit to the police that he was driving the vehicle, there must also be some evidence independent of the driver's admission because evidence of driving is an "essential element" of the crime. The driver's admission alone has been held insufficient to convict absent some corroboration.

Circumstantial evidence may be used to corroborate the driver's admission. For example, if the driver hit her head on the windshield upon impact, and there is blood matching the driver's blood type found on the glass, this may serve to corroborate the driver's admission. The independent evidence need not prove the act beyond a reasonable doubt provided it tends to confirm the driver's admission.

If the driver does not admit to driving the vehicle, circumstantial evidence may be the only evidence available to the prosecution, and has been held to be sufficient to convict in a drunk driving case. Convictions have been upheld in cases where, for example, the defendant was seen driving the vehicle a short time prior to the accident; or the defendant was found sleeping behind the wheel and the engine, although not running, was still warm.

TYPE OF VEHICLE

In general, all jurisdictions include automobiles, trucks and motorcycles as types of vehicles covered under their drunk driving law. Many jurisdictions parallel the language of the Uniform Vehicle Code, which simply uses the term "any vehicle":

> (a) A person shall not drive or be in actual physical control of *any vehicle* while (1) the alcohol concentration in such person's blood or breath is 0.08 or more . . .

One must also be aware of judicial interpretations of the statutory term. In general, if the statute uses the term "motor vehicle," it refers to vehicles which are equipped with a motor. Thus, less traditional forms of transportation, such as a a moped or snowmobile, may be covered under the statute. However, a statute which merely uses the term "vehicle," may be interpreted more broadly by a court to include a bicycle. In fact, a North Carolina court has interpreted its statute to prohibit drunken horseback riding.

LOCATION OF OFFENSE

Section 11-901.1(a) of the Uniform Vehicle Code makes it unlawful to drive drunk "within" or "in" the state. Many states also use this terminology in defining the places where drunk driving is prohibited. Because the intent is to protect the public from harm, the statutes generally apply to public highways and roads, and areas open to the public, including private property, such as parking lots.

For example, New York's drunk driving statute defines the applicable locations as follows:

> Where applicable. The provisions of this section shall apply upon public highways, private roads open to motor vehicle traffic and any other parking lot. For the purposes of this section "parking lot" shall mean any area or areas of private property, including a driveway, near or contiguous to and provided in connection with premises and used as a means of access to and egress from a public highway to such premises and having a capacity for the parking of four or more motor vehicles. The provisions of this section shall not apply to any area or areas of private property comprising all or part of property on which is situated a one or two family residence. (N.Y. Veh. & Traf. Law §1192(7)).

Some statutes do not specify locations where drunk driving is prohibited in the statute, relying on the language that drunk driving is prohibited anywhere "in the state." Such statutes have been interpreted literally and thus have resulted in drunk driving convictions regardless of the location provided the offense occurred within the state.

Unless the statute is one which does not specify actual locations where drunk driving is prohibited, the location of the offense is an element of the crime that must be proven by the prosecution. Generally, location is proven through eyewitness testimony or circumstantial evidence.

INTOXICATION WHILE DRIVING

It is not enough to merely establish that the driver was intoxicated. It is also necessary to establish that the driver was intoxicated *while* he or she was driving or operating the vehicle. For example, a driver involved in a one-car accident may claim that her intoxication resulted from her drinking after the accident occurred, particularly where considerable time has elapsed between the accident and the arrival of police.

INTENT

In order to convict, the prosecution does not have to prove that the driver had any specific intent—i.e., mens rea—to drive while intoxicated. Proof of a general intent to drink and then proceed to drive is all that is required. Thus, the driver need not be aware that he is under the influence of alcohol while driving in order to be convicted provided he consumed alcoholic beverages and thereafter intentionally drove.

BLOOD ALCOHOL CONCENTRATION (BAC) LEVEL

The primary indicator of whether a person has had too much to drink is their blood alcohol concentration (BAC) level. The BAC describes the concentration of alcohol in a person's blood expressed as weight per unit of volume. For example, at 0.10 percent BAC, there is a concentration of 100 mg of alcohol per 100 ml of blood. It is not necessary to obtain a blood sample to determine a driver's BAC level. Generally, the BAC level is measured by analyzing the driver's exhaled breath.

BAC measurements provide an objective way to identify levels of impairment, because alcohol concentration in the body is directly related to impairment. Because the rate that alcohol is absorbed into the blood differs from person to person based on such factors as age, weight and gender, the effect that alcohol will have on a particular person varies greatly. Other factors, such as the amount of food in the stomach, also affect alcohol absorption. Therefore, it is difficult to determine exactly how many drinks will result in a heightened BAC.

Some people erroneously believe that certain types of alcoholic beverages, such as beer and wine, are less intoxicating than hard liquor. However, impairment is not determined by the type of drink but by the amount of alcohol ingested over a specific period of time. For example, there is a comparable amount of alcohol in a 12-ounce glass of beer and 1.25 ounces of 80 proof liquor. In fact, beer is the most common drink consumed by people involved in alcohol-related crashes.

Studies have shown that alcohol may affect driving ability and crash likelihood at BAC levels as low as 0.02%. The probability of a crash begins to increase significantly at a BAC level of 0.05 percent, and climbs rapidly after about 0.08 percent. Statistics have demonstrated that a large percentage of drivers who are fatally injured have a BAC of at least 0.08 percent.

A table depicting the percent of fatally injured people with a BAC level of 0.08% or greater (1992-2002) is set forth at Appendix 16.

The push for a national 0.08 percent BAC limit was based on laboratory and on-road research which demonstrated that the majority of drivers, regardless of experience, are significantly impaired at 0.08 percent BAC, and show a critical decline in their ability to perform critical driving tasks, such as braking, steering, lane changing, judgment, and divided attention. In fact, research suggests that the most critical aspect of impairment is the reduction in the ability to handle several tasks at once, a skill motor vehicle drivers must perform.

For drivers age 35 and older with BACs at or above 0.15 percent on weekend nights, the likelihood of being killed in a single-vehicle crash is more than 380 times higher than it is for nondrinking drivers.

A table depicting the percent of fatally injured people with a BAC level of 0.15% or greater (1992-2002) is set forth at Appendix 17.

Although alcohol is known to increase crash likelihood, its presence is neither necessary nor sufficient to cause a crash. Every crash in which a driver has a high BAC is not caused by alcohol. However, the incidence of alcohol involvement is much lower in crashes involving nonfatal injuries, and it is lower still in crashes that do not involve injuries at all.

ILLEGAL PER SE STATUTES

Proof of intoxication generally requires the prosecutor to prove that the driver consumed enough alcohol to satisfy the jurisdiction's legal definition of intoxication. The first state laws prohibited driving while intoxicated without defining an illegal BAC level. Only obviously drunk drivers were likely to be arrested under those statutes, and convictions were difficult to obtain without an objective standard of measurement.

Once BAC levels were established to determine a degree of impairment, it became easier to prosecute offenders. At first, the BAC levels were used as presumptive evidence that the offender was impaired, and that presumption was rebuttable by the defendant.

Now, all jurisdictions have established an "illegal per se" BAC level. The statute sets a minimum BAC level—e.g. 0.08%—to satisfy the intoxication requirement. Thus, the prosecution does not have to prove that the driver was "intoxicated" or "under the influence," or that alcohol consumption had any effect on the driver's ability to operate the vehicle. The prosecutor need only prove that the defendant was driving with a BAC level at or above the illegal per se limit, even if the driver exhibited no visible signs of intoxication.

For example, New York's illegal per se statute states:

> Driving while intoxicated; per se. No person shall operate a motor vehicle while such person has .08 of one per centum or more by weight of alcohol in the person's blood as shown by chemical analysis of such person's blood, breath, urine or saliva, made pursuant to the provisions of section eleven hundred ninety-four of this article. (N.Y. Veh. & Traf. Law §1192(2)).

The Uniform Vehicle Code has also adopted 0.08 percent as the per se illegal BAC limit:

SECTION 11-902. Driving while under the influence of alcohol or drugs.

(a) A person shall not drive or be in actual physical control of any vehicle while:

1. The alcohol concentration in such person's blood or breath is 0.08 or more based on the definition of blood and breath units in §11-903(a) (5).

A "per se" violation needs no further corroboration. The BAC in and of itself is proof that the law was violated. Defendants can no longer try to prove they were not impaired, although they can challenge the validity of the BAC tests.

Presently, all 50 states and the District of Columbia have set their illegal per se BAC level at 0.08%, except Minnesota, which has maintained its illegal per se BAC limit at 0.10%. However, Minnesota has passed legislation to lower its BAC limit to 0.08% effective August 1, 2005.

A table depicting the illegal BAC levels, by state, is set forth at Appendix 18.

All states have "zero tolerance" laws that prohibit people younger than 21 from driving after drinking. Typically, these laws prohibit driving with a BAC of 0.02 percent or greater. The law as it pertains to young drivers is discussed more fully in Chapter 4 of this almanac.

CHAPTER 3:
BAC DETECTION METHODS

IN GENERAL

Although police cannot stop and test individual drivers without cause, they can investigate any driver who, based on established criteria, appears to have been driving while impaired by alcohol. As further set forth below, most alcohol-impaired driving arrests are made by officers on routine patrol who discern signs of impairment after stopping a driver for an ordinary traffic violation. This chapter discusses the right of law enforcement officers to stop drivers suspected of drinking and driving, and the testing methods law enforcement officers employ to determine whether a driver is alcohol-impaired.

CHEMICAL TESTING

The term *blood* alcohol concentration is somewhat misleading because a blood sample is not necessary to determine a person's BAC. The simplest way to test a person's BAC is by analyzing exhaled breath—a "breathalyzer" test—the primary method of testing used by law enforcement agencies. A person's BAC level can also be measured by testing their urine or saliva. Most states provide that any one of the foregoing samples is admissible as proof of intoxication.

For example, the Indiana drunk driving statute provides:

> Scope of Use of Chemical Test Results. At any proceeding concerning an offense under IC 9-30-5 or a violation under IC 9-30-15, evidence of the amount by weight of alcohol that was in the blood of the person charged with the offense (1) at the time of the alleged violation; or (2) within the time allowed for testing under IC 9-30-6-2, *as shown by an analysis of the person's breath, blood or urine or other bodily substance,* is admissible. (Ind. Code An. §9-30-6-3).

A passive alcohol sensor is a common device used by law enforcement officers at roadside stops. The passive alcohol sensor is non-invasive and can be performed even if the driver remains in his or her vehicle. Breath testing equipment is evaluated for precision and accuracy by the National Highway Traffic Safety Administration (NHTSA), and must be accurate within plus or minus .005 of the true BAC value to meet NHTSA approval.

Nevertheless, the most accurate and direct determination of one's BAC is obtained through an analysis of a blood sample. Advantages of a blood sample over other types of BAC testing is that it is relatively inexpensive and can be taken by a number of qualified persons who are generally available, there is reduced likelihood that the person administering the test can interfere with the results, and a blood sample, unlike a breath analysis, can be saved indefinitely. The disadvantages are that it takes longer to obtain the results of a blood test, and the procedure is more invasive and carries certain health risks.

IMPLIED CONSENT STATUTES AND THE REFUSAL TO SUBMIT TO BAC TESTING

A driver who has been drinking and is subsequently stopped for suspicion of drunk driving may be understandably reluctant to submit to BAC testing, because the results of the test may be all that is needed for a conviction. Because BAC testing provides a clear advantage to the prosecution, and assists states in making sure their roads are free from drunk drivers, implied consent laws have been enacted to deter the drunk driver's incentive to refuse to submit to BAC testing.

Implied consent statutes generally provide for automatic suspension of the license of any driver who refuses to submit to BAC testing. In some states, evidence of refusal is admissible at trial, and may be the basis for an enhanced sentence if the driver is convicted on the drunk driving offense. Nevertheless, an implied consent statute generally requires that the law enforcement officer have some reasonable basis or probable cause to believe that the driver was operating under the influence before he requests the driver to submit to a test.

Some states give drivers the statutory right to consult with an attorney before making the decision whether or not to submit to BAC testing. However, this right is not absolute and will be limited if the driver is unable to contact an attorney within a reasonable period of time. If, however, the police fail to advise the driver of his or her right to contact an attorney, in jurisdictions where notice is required, the results of any police-administered test may be suppressed.

A table of states which have enacted mandatory BAC level testing is set forth at Appendix 19.

Section 6-207 of the Uniform Vehicle Code sets forth a typical implied consent provision:

SECTION 6-207(a). Any person who operates a motor vehicle upon the highways of this State shall be deemed to have given consent, subject to the provisions of §11-903, to a test or tests of such operator's blood, breath, or urine for the purpose of determining operator's alcohol concentration or the presence of other drugs. The test or tests shall be administered at the direction of a law enforcement officer who has probable cause to believe the person has been violating §11-902(a), and one of the following conditions exists:

1. The person has been arrested for violating §11-902(a) or any other offense alleged to have been committed while the person was violating §11-902(a);

2. The person has been involved in an accident;

3. The person has refused to submit to the preliminary screening test authorized by §6-209; or

4. The person has submitted to the preliminary screening test authorized by §6-209 which disclosed an alcohol concentration of 0.08 or more.

Most jurisdictions provide that the license of a driver who refuses to submit to BAC testing is subject to mandatory suspension or revocation. The Uniform Vehicle Code also provides that drivers who refuse to submit to testing, or who have tested at or above 0.08 percent are subject to license revocation:

Section 6-207(c). A person requested to submit to a test as provided above shall be warned by the law enforcement officer requesting the test that a refusal to submit to the test will result in revocation of such person's license to operate a motor vehicle for (six months) (one year).

Suspensions are imposed primarily to protect the public from intoxicated drivers rather than merely a form of punishment for the driver. Although many offenders continue to drive after having their licenses suspended, many studies have indicated that the suspensions reduce recidivism compared with offenders whose licenses are not suspended. In addition, the reductions in violations and crashes associated with license suspension continue well beyond the suspension period.

DRIVER'S RIGHT TO CHEMICAL TEST

A sober driver accused of driving while impaired may wish to clear his name by obtaining an independent chemical test to use as exculpatory evidence of sobriety. Many states allow a driver to undergo a second test once he or she has submitted to the test requested by a law enforcement officer. Some states have held that a driver has the right to an independent test whether or not he or she submitted to the initial test. However, a police officer is generally not under any duty to advise the driver of his or her right to an independent test unless the statute explicitly requires him to do so.

The initial police-administered test is generally a breath test. However, the most common privately administered test is a blood test due to its accuracy. Unfortunately, as a practical matter, a driver who is arrested late at night may not be able to obtain a blood test. If the police give the driver the opportunity to obtain an independent test, but the driver is unable to do so, the initial police-administered test is nonetheless admissible against the driver.

For example, Alabama's drunk driving law provides:

> The person tested may at his own expense have a physician, or a qualified technician, registered nurse or other qualified person of his own choosing administer a chemical test or tests in addition to any administered at the discretion of a law enforcement officer. The failure or inability to obtain an additional test by a person shall not preclude the admission of evidence relating to the test or tests taken at the direction of a law enforcement officer. (Ala. Code 32-5-192).

Nevertheless, if the police refuse to allow the driver to obtain an independent test, the initial test results may not be admissible.

SOBRIETY CHECKPOINTS

Police are permitted to use roadblocks to stop drivers at specified locations to identify alcohol-impaired drivers. These locations are generally known as sobriety checkpoints. At the sobriety checkpoint, all drivers, or a predetermined proportion of them, are stopped based on rules that prevent police from arbitrarily selecting drivers. Sobriety checkpoints are often established at times when drinking and driving is most prevalent, such as weekends and certain holiday periods.

Sobriety checkpoints are a very visible enforcement method intended to deter potential offenders as well as to catch violators. Sobriety checkpoints that are well-publicized, and set up frequently over long enough periods, have proven to be effective deterrents to drivers who fear they will be apprehended if they drink and drive. Results from a 2002 study undertaken by the Centers for Disease Control (CDC) indicate that sobriety checkpoints consistently reduced alcohol-related crashes by about 20 percent.

According to the NHTSA, two-thirds of the driving age public believe sobriety checkpoints should be used more frequently than they are now. In fact, a majority of drivers who drink are supportive of increased use of sobriety checkpoints.

The U.S. Supreme Court held in 1990 that properly conducted sobriety checkpoints are legal under the federal Constitution. Most state courts that have addressed the issue have upheld checkpoints, too, but some have interpreted state law to prohibit sobriety checkpoints.

A table of states which have enacted sobriety checkpoint legislation is set forth at Appendix 20.

VISUAL DWI DETECTION OF MOVING VEHICLES

Unlike sobriety checkpoints, which stop all or a predetermined number of drivers regardless of any visual detection of alcohol impairment, law enforcement officers also routinely stop drivers who exhibit some indication of alcohol impairment while in motion, such as weaving or coming dangerously close to stationary objects or other vehicles. According to the NHTSA, the highest probability of alcohol impairment is associated with the actions of turning a vehicle with a wide radius or straddling a center or lane marker between the left-hand and right-hand wheels.

In addition, the law enforcement officer obtains visual cues from the manner of response when the officer requests the driver to pull over. For example, cues suggesting alcohol impairment may include a sudden stop, a swerve, contact with a stationary object, a slow or no response, or an attempt to evade police and flee the scene.

NHTSA RESEARCH AND DEVELOPMENT OF BAC EVALUATION METHODS

An emphasis on DWI enforcement over the last two decades has resulted in a significant improvement in traffic safety, as demonstrated by a reduction in overall traffic accidents as well as those which are alcohol-related. The NHTSA has made a large contribution to this reduction in DWI by providing law enforcement officers with scientifically valid and useful information and training materials concerning DWI behaviors. In 1975, the NHTSA began sponsoring research that led to the development of standardized methods for police officers to use when evaluating drivers who are suspected of driving while impaired.

This information is the product of research sponsored by the NHTSA, which led to the development of a DWI detection guide listing 20 driving cues and the probabilities that a driver exhibiting one or more of those cues would have a BAC of at least .010 percent. A similar study recently sponsored by the NHTSA identified 24 driving cues that predict DWI at the 0.08 percent BAC level. The NHTSA has also sponsored research that led to the development of a motorcycle DWI detection guide.

In 1981, law enforcement officers began using the NHTSA's Standardized Field Sobriety Test (SFST) battery to help determine whether drivers who are suspected of DWI have blood alcohol concentrations (BACs) greater than 0.10 percent. An evaluation of a number of tests routinely given by law enforcement officers at roadside stops was made, including, for example, the finger to nose test, maze tracing, and counting backward, in addition to the driver's reaction to central nervous system depressants, known as horizontal gaze nystagmus (HGN), which is more fully described below.

Statistically, HGN tested to be the most predictive of the individual measures studied. However, the combined scores of three of the tests studied—one-leg stand, walk and turn, and horizontal gaze nystagmus—provided a slightly higher correlation to BAC than HGN alone. The combined score correctly discriminated between BACs below or above 0.10 percent in 83% of the subjects tested in the study conducted in 1977.

Upon receiving these results, the NHTSA sponsored a subsequent study to standardize the test administration and scoring procedures and conduct further evaluations of the new battery of the three tests. The research demonstrated that police officers tended to increase their arrest rates and were more effective in estimating BACs of stopped drivers after they had been trained in the administration and scoring of the Standardized Field Sobriety Test (SFST) battery.

The results of the study were documented in detail in a report entitled *Development and Field Test of Psychophysical Tests for DWI Arrest* (Tharp, Burns and Moskowitz, 1981), which has been cited numerous times throughout the United States to establish the scientific validity of the SFST battery and to support law enforcement officers' in-court testimony.

THE STANDARDIZED FIELD SOBRIETY TEST

As discussed above, the Standardized Field Sobriety Test (SFST) has largely replaced the invalidated performance tests once used by police officers in traffic stops to make DWI arrest decisions, and is used in all 50 states. The SFST has become the standard pre-arrest procedure for evaluating DWI by most law enforcement agencies. The SFST accurately and reliably assists trained officers in making DWI arrest decisions at 0.08 percent BAC. The SFST has also proven to be useful for making arrest decisions at 0.04 percent BAC.

As set forth above, the SFST consists of a battery of three tests which are administered and evaluated in a standardized manner to obtain valid indicators of impairment and establish probable cause for arrest: (i) horizontal gaze nystagmus (HGN); (ii) walk-and-turn; and (iii) one-leg stand.

The Horizontal Gaze Nystagmus (HGN)

Horizontal gaze nystagmus (HGN) is an involuntary jerking of one's eye that occurs naturally as the eyes gaze to the side. Under normal conditions, nystagmus occurs when the eyes are rotated at high peripheral angles. However, when a person is impaired by alcohol, nystagmus is exaggerated and may occur at lesser angles. Studies have indicated that there are consistent changes in HGN with increasing doses of alcohol.

An alcohol-impaired person will also often have difficulty smoothly tracking a moving object. In the HGN test, the officer observes the eyes of the driver as he or she follows a slowly moving object horizontally with his or her eyes. The examiner looks for three indicators of impairment in each eye:

1. If the eye cannot follow a moving object smoothly;

2. If jerking is distinct when the eye is at maximum deviation; and

3. If the angle of onset of jerking is within 45 degrees of center.

If, between the two eyes, four or more clues appear, the suspect is likely to have a BAC of 0.10 percent or greater. NHTSA research indicates that the HGN test allows proper classification of approximately 77 percent of suspects. HGN may also indicate consumption of seizure medications, phencyclidine, and a variety of inhalants, barbiturates and other depressants.

Many law enforcement officers consider the HGN test a foolproof method to provide indisputable evidence of alcohol in a driver's system. Unlike performance tests, which result in uncertainties due to the normal variation in human physical and cognitive capabilities, most experienced drinkers cannot conceal the physiological effects of alcohol from an officer trained in HGN administration. HGN is an involuntary reaction over which an individual has no control whatsoever.

Walk and Turn Test

The walk-and-turn test, as well as the one-leg stand test which is discussed below, are easily performed by most unimpaired people. They merely require a suspect to listen to and follow instructions while performing simple physical movements. However, when an individual is impaired, he or she has difficulty performing tasks which require their attention to be divided between simple mental and physical exercises.

During the walk-and-turn test, the driver is asked to take nine steps, heel to toe, along a straight line. After taking the steps, the driver must turn on one foot and return in the same manner in the opposite direction. The examiner looks for eight indicators of impairment, including:

1. If the suspect cannot keep his balance while listening to the instructions;

2. If the suspect begins before the instructions are finished;

3. If the suspect stops while walking to regain his balance;

4. If the suspect does not touch heel-to-toe;

5. If the suspect steps off the line;

6. If the suspect uses his or her arms to balance;

7. If the suspect makes an improper turn; or

8. If the suspect takes an incorrect number of steps.

The NHTSA research indicates that 68 percent of individuals who exhibit two or more indicators in the performance of the test will have a BAC of 0.10 percent or greater.

One Leg Stand

The one leg stand requires the driver to stand with one foot approximately six inches off the ground and count aloud by thousands until told to put his or her foot down. The officer times the driver for 30 seconds and looks for four indicators of impairment, including (I) swaying while balancing; (ii) using arms to balance; (iii) hopping to maintain balance; and (iv) putting one's foot down. NHTSA research indicates that 76 percent of individuals who exhibit two or more such indicators in the performance of the test will have a BAC of 0.10 of greater.

PASSIVE ALCOHOL SENSORS

Passive alcohol sensors identify alcohol in the exhaled breath near a driver's mouth. They are particularly effective in situations where the driver is able to effectively hide symptoms of impairment for short periods of time. Because passive alcohol sensors are not intrusive, they have been held not to violate the constitutional prohibitions against unreasonable search and seizure.

Studies conducted by the Insurance Institute for Highway Safety (IIHS) have indicated that police using these sensors were able to detect more offenders compared with officers who did not use the sensors. Police without sensors detected 55 percent of drivers whose BACs were at or above 0.10 percent whereas police with sensors successfully detected 71 percent of the drivers with illegal BACs.

ALTERNATIVE TESTING METHODS

In some cases involving disabled drivers, the individual cannot perform the standardized tests. In these cases, some other battery of tests such as counting aloud, reciting the alphabet, or finger dexterity tests may be administered. Several appellate court decisions, however, have indicated that if a police officer administers a test that requires a subject who is in custody to respond orally in other than a routine information-giving fashion—e.g., by asking them to indicate the date of their sixth birthday—the subject should be given their Miranda warning first as the information being sought may be considered testimonial or communicative in nature.

CHAPTER 4:
UNDERAGE DRINKING AND DRIVING

TEENAGE DRIVERS

As a group, teenage drivers are disproportionately involved in motor vehicle crashes worldwide. Although teenagers drive less than all but the oldest drivers, their numbers of crashes and crash deaths are disproportionately high. The risk of crash involvement per mile driven among 16-19 years-old is 4 times the risk among older drivers. Risk is highest at age 16. In fact, the crash rate per mile driven is almost 3 times as high among 16 year-olds as it is among 18-19 year-olds. According to a 1999 Highway Loss Data Institute study, losses for cars insured for teenagers to drive are more than double those of cars insured for use by adults only.

Crash rates among young drivers are high largely because of their immaturity combined with driving inexperience. Teenagers engage in risky driving practices, such as speeding and tailgating, and they are less likely to wear safety belts. In addition, a teenager's lack of experience behind the wheel makes it difficult for them to recognize and respond to hazards.

Teenagers not only have higher crash rates than other age groups, their crashes are different. Analyses of fatal crash data indicate that teenage drivers are more likely to be at fault in their crashes, which are more likely to involve speeding, driver error, single-vehicle crashes, and the highest vehicle occupancy crashes.

TEENAGE PASSENGERS

In addition to teenage drivers, many teenagers die as passengers in motor vehicles driven by other teenagers. Sixty-one percent of teenage passenger deaths in 2002 occurred in crashes in which another teenager was driving. Teenagers far exceed all other age groups in terms of per capita deaths as both drivers and passengers, but their passenger fatality rates are much more extreme compared with those of older drivers. Among teenage drivers, 16 year-olds have by far the highest rates of teenage passenger deaths in their vehicle per licensed driver and per mile driven. Passenger vehicle death rates per 100,000 people in 2002 peaked at age 19 for drivers and at age 18 for passengers.

RECENT STATISTICS

The following statistics have been compiled from the U.S. Department of Transportation and the National Transportation Safety Administration:

In 2002, 5,933 teenagers died in the United States from motor vehicle crash injuries. Although this is 32 percent fewer than in 1975, teenage crash deaths in 2002 were 6 percent higher than in 2001.

Teenagers accounted for 10 percent of the U.S. population in 2002 and 14 percent of motor vehicle deaths. They represented 16 percent of passenger vehicle occupant deaths in 2002, 7 percent of pedestrian deaths, 5 percent of motorcycle deaths, and 13 percent of bicycle deaths.

Eighty-seven percent of teen motor vehicle deaths in 2002 were passenger vehicle occupants. The rest were pedestrians (6%), motorcyclists (3%), bicyclists (2%), and people in other kinds of vehicles (3%).

Motor vehicle crashes are the number one cause of death among 16-19 year olds. Forty percent of deaths of 16-19 year-olds in 2000 from all causes occurred in crashes.

Forty-six percent of females ages 16-19 who died in 2000 were involved in a motor vehicle crash. This compares with 37 percent of teenage male deaths.

Fifty-two percent of teenage motor vehicle deaths in 2002 occurred on Friday, Saturday, and Sunday.

Forty-one percent of teenage motor vehicle deaths in 2002 occurred between 9 pm and 6 am.

About 2 out of every 3 teenagers killed in motor vehicle crashes in 2002 were males.

Since 1975, teenage motor vehicle deaths have decreased more among males (40%) than among females (9%).

Population-based death rates among drivers aged 16-19 peaked at age 19 for males (28 per 100,000 people) and at age 18 for females (12 per 100,000 people). Death rates among teenage passengers peaked at age 18 for both males (15 per 100,000 people) and females (9 per 100,000 people).

The rate of nighttime fatal crashes per 100 million miles traveled in 2001 by male drivers 16-19 years old was about 5 times the rate for 30-54-year-old male drivers. The corresponding comparison for females is 4 times the rate.

More than half of teenage passenger vehicle occupant deaths in 2002 were drivers (55 percent), and less than half were passengers (45 percent).

Sixty-one percent of teenage passenger deaths in 2002 occurred in crashes in which another teenager was driving. Among people of all ages, 20 percent of passenger deaths in 2002 occurred when a teenager was driving.

ALCOHOL USE AS A FACTOR IN AUTOMOBILE ACCIDENTS

Alcohol use is the number one drug problem among young people. Although studies show that young drivers are less likely than adults to drive after drinking alcohol, their crash risks are substantially higher when they do. This is especially true at low and moderate blood alcohol concentrations (BACs) and is thought to result from teenagers' combined inexperience with both drinking and driving.

According to the NHTSA, more than 40% of all 16-20 year old deaths result from motor vehicle crashes, and approximately one-half of those accidents are alcohol-related. The total number of young drivers aged 16-20 involved in fatal crashes decreased marginally from 2000 to 2001. The number of young drivers who were intoxicated also decreased marginally. In 2001, the percent of intoxicated drivers among younger drivers involved in fatal crashes ranged from 8 percent for 16-year old drivers, to 26 percent for 20-year old drivers.

In 2002, 24% of drivers ages 15 to 20 who died in motor vehicle crashes had been drinking alcohol, and 25 percent of fatally injured 16-20-year-old passenger vehicle drivers had high blood alcohol concentrations—i.e., 0.08 percent or more. Teenage drivers with BACs in the 0.05-0.08 percent range are far more likely than sober teenage drivers to be killed in single-vehicle crashes—17 times more likely for males, 7 times more likely for females. At BACs of 0.08-0.10, risks are even higher, 52 times for males, 15 times for females.

A table depicting the percent of fatally injured passenger vehicle drivers age 16-20 with a BAC level of 0.08% or greater (1992-2002) is set forth at Appendix 21.

MINIMUM ALCOHOL PURCHASING AGE LAWS

Minimum alcohol purchasing age laws have been effective in reducing alcohol-related automobile accidents involving teenagers, and many communities are strengthening enforcement of these laws. For a long time, the legal age for purchasing alcohol was 21 years old in the majority of states. Then, in the 1960s and early 1970s, many states lowered their minimum purchasing ages to 18 or 19 years old.

According to the Insurance Institute for Highway Safety, the consequences of this action resulted in an increase in the number of 15-20 year-olds involved in nighttime fatal crashes. As a result of this and other studies with similar findings, a number of states raised their minimum alcohol purchasing ages. Some states reverted back to 21 years old, and other states set 19 or 20 as the minimum age. Subsequent research indicated that states which raised their minimum legal alcohol purchasing age experienced a 13 percent reduction in nighttime driver fatal crash involvement involving teenagers.

In 1984, 23 states had minimum alcohol purchasing ages of 21 years old. Federal legislation was enacted to withhold highway funds from the remaining 27 states if they did not follow suit. By 1988, all 50 states and the District of Columbia had raised their minimum alcohol purchasing age to 21 years old.

According to the NHTSA, fatal crashes among young drivers declined dramatically after states adopted the minimum purchasing age, and by 1996 the statistic had declined to 24 percent, the biggest improvement for any age group. In fact, between 1985 and 1995, the proportion of drivers aged 16-20 who were involved in fatal crashes, and were intoxicated, dropped 47 percent, the largest decrease or any age group during this period.

The NHTSA estimates that these laws have reduced traffic fatalities involving drivers 18 to 20 years old by 13 percent and have saved an estimated 21,887 lives since 1975. In 2002 alone, an estimated 917 lives were saved by minimum drinking age laws.

A table depicting the cumulative estimated number of lives saved by minimum age drinking laws from 1975 to 2002 is set forth at Appendix 22.

ZERO TOLERANCE LAWS

Zero tolerance laws make it illegal for drivers under the age of 21 to drive with any measurable amount of alcohol in their system, despite the BAC limit established for older drivers.

A table depicting the alcohol involvement among drivers age 16 to 20 in 2001, by age and BAC level, is set forth at Appendix 23.

The reasoning and justification behind zero tolerance laws is the illegality of persons under the age of 21 to purchase or publicly possess alcohol. If it is illegal for them to purchase or possess alcohol, they certainly should not be permitted to drive after having consumed alcohol. This is particularly troublesome due to the fact that young drivers are already more likely to be involved in automobile accidents due to other factors, such as lack of experience.

Federal legislation required all states to enact zero tolerance laws for youth by October 1, 1998 or face federal sanctions. As a result, all 50 states and the District of Columbia now have zero tolerance laws.

A table setting forth the zero tolerance BAC limit for each state is set forth at Appendix 24.

New York's drunk driving statute contains a typical "illegal per se" provision relating to young drivers:

> SECTION 1192-a. Operating a motor vehicle after having consumed alcohol; under the age of twenty-one; per se.
>
> No person under the age of twenty-one shall operate a motor vehicle after having consumed alcohol as defined in this section. For purposes of this section, a person under the age of twenty-one is deemed to have consumed alcohol only if such person has .02 of one per centum or more . . . of alcohol in the person's blood, as shown by chemical analysis of such person's blood, breath, urine or saliva, made pursuant to the provisions of section eleven hundred ninety-four of this article.

License suspension or revocation, or some other statutorily prescribed penalty may result if the driver's BAC level tests at or above the reduced blood alcohol concentration levels. Early research from states where a zero tolerance policy has been implemented indicates it might reduce teenagers' nighttime fatal crashes.

In most states, a young driver is deemed to have given his or her consent to BAC testing. This is known as an "implied consent" provision. The Uniform Vehicle Code sets forth a typical implied consent provision concerning BAC testing of drivers under the age of 21:

> Section 6-208(b). Any person under age (21) who drives or is in actual physical control of any vehicle upon the highways of this State shall be deemed to have given consent, subject to the provisions of §11-903, to a test or tests of such person's blood, breath, or urine for the purpose of determining such person's alcohol concentration or the presence of other drugs . . .

The Uniform Vehicle Code further provides that, if the young driver either refuses to submit to the test, or tests at or above the established limit, his or her license will be revoked:

> Section 6-208(d). A person under age (21) requested to submit to a test as provided above shall be warned by the law enforcement officer requesting the test that a refusal to submit to the test will result in revocation of such person's license to operate a vehicle for (six months) (one year). Following this warning, if a person under arrest refuses upon the request of a law enforcement officer to submit to a test designated by the law enforcement agency as provided in paragraph (b) of this section, none shall be given.

> Section 6-208(e). If the person under the age (21) refuses testing or submits to a test which discloses an alcohol concentration of any measurable and detectable amount under this section, the law enforcement officer shall submit a sworn report to the department, certifying that the test was requested pursuant to subsection (b) and that the person refused to submit to testing or submitted to a test which disclosed an alcohol concentration of any measurable and detectable amount.

> Section 6-208(f). Upon receipt of the sworn report of a law enforcement officer submitted under subsection (e), the department shall revoke the driver's license of the person for the periods specified in §6-214.

GRADUATED LICENSING

Until the mid 1990s, most states allowed teens to get full-privilege licenses at an early age, and little driving experience was required prior to licensure. For example, in 1995, only 30 states required a learner's permit, and only 11 required the permit to be held for a minimum period, ranging from 14 to 90 days. The result was a greatly elevated crash risk among young drivers. As more and more states adopt graduated licensing systems, which phase in full driving privileges, the crash problem is expected to decrease. Presently, the majority of states now have a three-stage "graduated licensing" system for young drivers.

A table of state laws pertaining to young drivers is set forth at Appendix 25.

Graduated licensing refers to the gradual advancement of a beginning young driver to an unrestricted driver, introducing beginners into the driving population in a low-risk manner. Under a graduated licensing system, the young driver is restricted from certain driving activities, such as driving at night or a limitation on passengers in the vehicle. In addition, special sanctions may be assessed to deter problems such as alcohol violations, speeding or other moving violations, and seat belt law violations. Those penalties may include an extension of the restricted driving period, or license suspension.

There are three stages to a full graduated system, and beginners must remain in each of the first two stages for set minimum time periods:

(1) supervised learner's period;

(2) intermediate license after the driver test is passed which limits unsupervised driving in high-risk situations; and

(3) a license with full privileges.

Key elements of the intermediate stage include limits on late-night unsupervised driving and transporting teenage passengers.

According to the model graduated licensing system developed by the National Committee on Uniform Traffic Laws and Ordinances (NCUTLO), violation of a state's "zero tolerance" law would prohibit a young driver from applying for an unrestricted license.

Graduated licensing systems have been shown to reduce crashes substantially unlike high school driver education and alcohol awareness programs, which have had little or no effect in reducing crashes per licensed driver. Although high school driver education programs can successfully teach driving skills, and programs warning against alcohol-impaired driving can impart knowledge about this behavior, teenage attitudes seem to be largely unaffected by such programs. This may be attributable to certain personality traits exhibited by teenagers, including rebelliousness, risk-taking, independence, defiance of authority; deviant driving practices, e.g. speeding; and drug and alcohol use.

PARENTAL LIABILITY

If an child under the age of 21 drinks and drives, their parent or legal guardian may be liable if the child is responsible for causing damage, injury or death. If the adult purchased or provided the alcohol, his or her liability would be even greater. The consumption or possession of alcohol by the child would subject the adult to criminal prosecution and civil suit.

Most states recognize the right of a parent to serve their own underage children alcoholic beverages in the privacy of their home, however, they are not allowed to provide their children alcohol to be consumed elsewhere, nor are they permitted to serve alcohol to other underage children, even in their own home.

Nevertheless, according to a 1993 report by the Johnson Institute ("Johnson Report"), when school-age youth are allowed to drink alcohol at home, they are not only more likely to use alcohol and other drugs outside the home, they are more likely to develop serious behavioral and health problems related to their use of alcohol and other drugs. The Johnson Report also indicates that when parents "bargain" with their underage children—i.e., they allow them to drink as long as they promise not to drink and drive—they are more likely to drive after drinking or be in a vehicle driven by someone who has been drinking.

Social host liability laws hold adults liable for providing alcohol to minors who are not their own children. This is particularly so if a child who is intoxicated causes damage, injury or death, or commits a crime.

State social host liability laws generally provide that adults who provide alcohol to underage drinkers, or who knowingly allow underage alcohol use in their home, can face jail time and/or a substantial monetary fine. In addition, if there are injuries or damages resulting from the minor's underage drinking, the adult will be liable for all such costs.

Thus, parents are advised to make sure there is adult supervision for all children who gather in their homes, particularly when there are teenage parties being held in the home. In addition, any alcohol kept in the home should be placed in a locked, secure location. Also, an adult should never purchase alcohol on behalf of a minor or they risk facing criminal and civil penalties.

CHAPTER 5:
DETERRENCE AND
ENFORCEMENT MEASURES

IN GENERAL

According to the National Highway Traffic Safety Administration (NHTSA), almost 75% of Americans think penalties for drinking and driving should be more severe. This chapter explores some of the penalties devised to deter drunk driving. A thorough understanding of the range of penalties a jurisdiction may impose is imperative for an individual being prosecuted for drunk driving. Such penalties may include a fine; imprisonment; license suspension or revocation; and mandatory alcohol or drug abuse treatment. The reader is thus advised to consult his or her jurisdiction's statute for specific sentencing provisions.

ADMINISTRATIVE LICENSE SUSPENSION

Among the most effective penalties designed to deter drinking and driving is the administrative license suspension (ALS), also referred to in some jurisdictions as administrative license revocation. ALS laws give state officials the authority to administratively suspend the license of any driver who either fails a BAC test, or refuses to submit to the test. Because administrative licensing action is triggered by failing or refusing to take a chemical test—not by conviction—anyone arrested is immediately subject to suspension, and notice of the suspension is given to the driver immediately. Thus, ALS laws remove impaired drivers from the road quickly, and virtually ensure that penalties will be applied. According to a 2001 survey conducted by the Insurance Research Council, 89 percent of respondents support ALS laws.

A table of state administrative license suspension provisions is set forth at Appendix 26.

In some states, the notice of suspension also serves as a temporary permit. Depending on the state, this permit may be valid for 7 to 90 days, during which time the suspension may be appealed. If there is no appeal, or if the appeal is not upheld, the license is suspended for a prescribed period of time. The length of suspension varies by state, from 2 days to a year for first-time offenders, but most commonly lasts 90 days. Longer suspensions are specified for repeat violators. Extended periods of license suspension may be expected to have stronger deterrent effects, while those of short duration may have very limited effects. The NHTSA recommends that ALS laws impose at least a 90-day suspension or a 30-day suspension followed by 60 days of restricted driving.

The success of laws against alcohol-impaired driving depends largely on deterrence, or keeping potential offenders off the road in the first place. A well-publicized and enforced ALS law increases public perception that punishment for alcohol-impaired driving is likely to occur and will be swiftly applied and appropriately severe—a perception that is necessary to deter potential offenders. It is important to note that ALS laws do not replace criminal prosecution, which is handled separately through the courts.

Constitutional Considerations

Courts have held that although licenses are taken prior to a hearing, due process is provided because ALS laws allow for prompt post-suspension hearings. People whose licenses are suspended have the right to an administrative hearing to determine the validity of the arrest and any alcohol testing.

Defendants have claimed that the double jeopardy clause of the U.S. Constitution prohibits the state from prosecuting an offender whose license has been suspended under an ALS law. But high courts in several states have found that a criminal prosecution following ALS does not violate the double jeopardy clause.

Cost-Benefit Analysis

ALS laws are not costly to enforce. In most states, drivers who have their licenses suspended must pay a reinstatement fee to receive a new license at the end of the suspension period. These fees, which are paid by offenders and not taxpayers, can cover or exceed the cost of the program. In addition, states which implement ALS laws gain additional funds by qualifying for federal safety incentive grants.

An NHTSA study of three state programs found not only that direct revenues exceeded expenses, but also that state costs associated with nighttime crashes declined dramatically. A study conducted by the Insurance Institute for Highway Safety found that ALR laws reduce the number of drivers involved in fatal crashes by about 9 percent during the high-risk nighttime hours. According to the NHTSA, among the 17 states implementing ALS either alone or in combination with other laws, the median effect is a 6 percent decrease in crashes likely to be alcohol-related.

POST-CONVICTION LICENSE SUSPENSION AND REVOCATION

Offenders also face license suspension or revocation upon conviction for a drunk driving offense, whether or not they are sentenced to imprisonment. The majority of jurisdictions impose mandatory suspensions or revocations following conviction. The severity of the penalty oftentimes depends on whether it was the driver's first offense or whether he or she is a repeat offender.

The Uniform Vehicle Code sets forth a typical license revocation provision:

Section 6-206. Mandatory revocation of license by department.

The department shall forthwith revoke the license of any driver upon receiving a record of such driver's conviction of any of the following offenses:

2. Driving or being in actual physical control of a motor vehicle while under the influence of alcohol or any drug as prohibited by §11-902.

Restricted Licenses

Because license suspension is an extreme hardship on individuals who rely on driving as their primary means of making a livelihood, many states restore driving privileges during suspension by issuing a restricted or conditional license. Also known as a hardship license, the restricted license permits the offender to drive with a suspended license under limited circumstances, such as to and from work.

A table of state laws concerning restoration of driving privileges during suspension is set forth at Appendix 27.

DRIVER ALCOHOL EDUCATION PROGRAMS—FIRST TIME OFFENDERS

Most states require a first time drunk driving offender to participate in an alcohol education program. A defendant may be able to work out a deal whereby his fine or license suspension period are reduced provided he successfully completes such a program. A driver alcohol education program is designed to eliminate or reduce recidivism amongst drunk drivers; diagnose and recommend treatment; provide information about alcohol and/or drug abuse and increase awareness about the dangers of combining substance abuse and driving. Research has shown driver education programs may have a small, positive effect on the subsequent behavior of first offenders and non-problem drinkers unlike multiple offenders and problem drinkers.

LICENSE PLATE SANCTIONS

Many states have enacted laws which authorize the police to impound a drunk driver's license plates and revoke his or registration, including Arizona, Arkansas, Delaware, Indiana, Kansas, Maine, Maryland, Michigan, Minnesota, New Hampshire, New York, North Dakota, Ohio, Oregon, Rhode Island, South Dakota, Virginia and Wyoming. Under the Uniform Vehicle Code, conviction of the following offenses may result in license plate impoundment and registration revocation:

Section 17-301. Suspension of registration.

Upon conviction of any of the following offenses the court may, in addition to other penalties prescribed by this code, suspend the registration of any vehicle or vehicles registered in the name of the person convicted for a period of not to exceed [period of time] and any such suspension shall be immediately reported by the court to the department:

1. Homicide by vehicle (manslaughter resulting from the operation of a motor vehicle);

2. Driving or being in actual physical control of a motor vehicle while under the influence of alcohol or any drug;

3. Any felony in the commission of which a motor vehicle is used;

4. Failure to stop, render aid or identify oneself as required by §10-102 in the event of a motor vehicle accident resulting in death or personal injury;

5. Unauthorized use of a motor vehicle belonging to another;

6. Driving while the privilege to do so is suspended or revoked;

7. Racing on a highway;

8. Willfully fleeing from or attempting to elude a police officer; or

9. Any offense punishable under §17-201.

A table of states with vehicle license plate confiscation laws is set forth at Appendix 28.

IGNITION INTERLOCKS

Forty-three states permit some offenders to drive only if their vehicles have been equipped with ignition interlocks. These devices analyze a driver's breath and disable the ignition if the driver has been drinking. Ignition interlock devices analyze a driver's breath and disable the ignition if the driver has been drinking. Before starting the car, the driver must blow a sample of breath into the device. If the driver's BAC level is below a specific limit, the engine will start. The car will not start if the BAC level exceeds the specified limit. Ignition interlock devices are generally intended for repeat and chronic drunk drivers, although they are authorized in some jurisdictions for first time offenders.

A table of states with laws requiring ignition interlock devices is set forth at Appendix 29.

VEHICLE IMMOBILIZATION

Some states have enacted laws which prevent an individual convicted of drunk driving from operating their vehicle by immobilizing it. This may be accomplished by placing a wheel lock—also known as a boot—on the car, or by installing a locking device on the steering wheel

VEHICLE IMPOUNDMENT/FORFEITURE

When an individual is arrested on a drunk driving charge, his or her vehicle is generally impounded overnight. In 30 states, repeat or multiple offenders may forfeit vehicles that are driven while impaired by alcohol.

In 1999, New York City became the first jurisdiction to enact a law authorizing both the seizure and forfeiture of cars belonging to first-time drunk driving offenders. The policy is based on the city's forfeiture law, which allows police to seize any weapon used in a crime. It is intended to lower New York City's drunken-driving fatalities. Last year, 31 people were killed in the city as a result of drunken driving. New York City is the first to use a city forfeiture law to seize vehicles for drunk driving. In 23 other U.S. states, there are laws that allow police to confiscate or impound cars of drunken drivers, but they usually apply only to repeat offenders.

Under the New York law, a driver suspected of driving while intoxicated may be stopped and required to take a breath test. If the driver has a BAC level of 0.08 or higher, he will be arrested and his car seized. Drivers whose BAC is lower than 0.08 may be arrested for driving while impaired, but will not lose their car. Drivers who refuse to take the breath test can be charged with drunk driving and lose their cars based on the police officer's assessment of their behavior. Once an arrest for drunk driving is made and the car is seized, there will follow both a criminal case against the drunk driver and a civil case seeking forfeiture of the vehicle.

A table of states with vehicle forfeiture laws is set forth at Appendix 30.

PUBLIC HUMILIATION

Some jurisdictions have resorted to public humiliation as a means to deter drunk driving. For example, the drunk driver may be required to place an ad in the newspaper, a bumper sticker on his or her car, or wear a sign announcing their drunk driving behavior. The reasoning behind public humiliation is that since it is such a strong deterrent, it may make some offenders less likely to repeat the offense.

Public shaming has been used for several years in lower courts. Some federal courts have followed the lead of lower courts and ordered guilty parties to announce their wrongdoing to the public, e.g., by newspaper ads and bumper stickers. For example, a district judge in Troy, Michigan ordered drunken drivers to attach bumper stickers to their cars that read: "Drunk Driving, you can't afford it." A Houston, Texas court sentenced a drunk driver to carry a sign outside a bar for five days announcing he killed two people while driving drunk.

IMPRISONMENT

Sentencing structure among the states varies, thus, it would not be possible to set forth the penalties in detail in this almanac. The reader is advised to check the law of his or her jurisdiction for specific sentencing limitations. As an example, the Alabama sentencing statute for DWI offenders (Ala. Code §32-5A-191) provides for a graduated increase in prison sentences depending on the number of offenses committed in a 5-year period:

First offense: Imprisonment for not more than 1 year. . .

Second offense within 5 years: Imprisonment, which may include hard labor, in a county or municipal jail for not more than 1 year. . .

Third offense within 5 years: 60 days (mandatory) to 1 year imprisonment, which may include hard labor, in county or municipal jail. . .

Fourth or subsequent offense within 5 years (Class C Felony): 1 year and 1 day (mandatory) to 10 years imprisonment, which may include hard labor for the county or state . . .

Some jurisdictions have adopted sentencing "guidelines" for a judge to follow, which establish a sentencing range based on certain aggravating and mitigating factors. Section 11-902 of the Uniform Vehicle Code sets forth the following penalties:

Section 11-902. Driving while under the influence of alcohol or drugs.

(c) In addition to the provisions of §11-904, every person convicted of violating this section shall be punished by imprisonment for not less than 10 days or more than one year, or by fine of not less than $100 nor more than $1,000, or by both such fine and imprisonment and on a second or subsequent conviction, such person shall be punished by imprisonment for not less than 90 days nor more than one year, and, in the discretion of the court, a fine of not more than $1,000.

A table of states with mandatory imprisonment provisions for a first DWI conviction is set forth at Appendix 31.

In addition, many states which do not impose imprisonment on first-time offenders do require mandatory sentences of imprisonment for drivers convicted of second or subsequent drunk driving offenses. Harsher penalties are assessed if the driver is determined to be a "habitual offender," which may include commitment to a drug treatment facility.

For example, the Uniform Vehicle Code provides:

Section 11-904. Post-conviction examination and remedies.

(b) In addition to the penalties imposed by §11-902(c), and after receiving the results of the examination in subsection (a) or, upon a hearing and determination that the person is an *habitual user* of alcohol or other drugs, the court may order supervised treatment on an outpatient basis, or upon additional determinations that the person constitutes a danger to self or others and that adequate treatment facilities are available, the court may order such person committed for treatment at a facility or institution approved by the (State Department of Health).

A table of states with mandatory imprisonment provisions for repeat DWI convictions is set forth at Appendix 32.

THE NATIONAL DRIVER REGISTER

The National Driver Register (NDR), is a computerized database of information about drivers who have had their licenses revoked or suspended, or who have been convicted of serious traffic violations such as driving while impaired by alcohol or drugs.

State motor vehicle agencies provide the NDR with the names of individuals who have lost their driving privilege, or who have been convicted of a serious traffic violation. When a person applies for a driver's license the state checks to see if the name is in the NDR files. If a person has been reported to the NDR as a problem driver, the license may be denied.

Authorized Recipients

The following individuals are legally authorized to receive information from the NDR:

1. Any individual under the provisions of the Privacy Act;

2. State and federal driver's license officials;

3. Current or prospective employers of motor vehicle operators;

4. Air carriers for pilot applicants;

5. The Federal Railroad Administration and employers of railroad engineers;

6. The Federal Aviation Administration for airmen medical certification;

7. The U.S. Coast Guard for merchant mariner certification; and

8. The National Transportation Safety Board and the Federal Highway Administration for accident investigations.

Individual's Right of Access to Information

An individual is entitled, under the provisions of the Privacy Act, to request a file search to see if he or she has a file with the NDR. In order to access this information, the individual must fill out an *Individual Request Form* and mail it or take it to their local motor vehicle agency. For a small fee, they will forward the request to the NDR.

A copy of the Individual NDR File Request Form is set forth at Appendix 33.

Employer Inquiries

An employer who employs motor vehicle operators may wish to request an NDR file check on current or prospective employees as part of their safety program provided the employee is seeking employment, or is already employed, as a driver.

In order to obtain this information, the employee may go to the local motor vehicle agency and ask for an NDR file check. For this purpose, a *Current or Prospective Employee Form* must be completed by the employee and submitted to the state in which the employee is licensed.

Any information sent to the employer from the NDR should also be given to the employee.

If the employee does have an NDR file, the NDR will provide the employer with the name of the state, and the address and telephone number in order to request a copy of the driver record to verify that it is the same individual. Any information on the NDR file that was reported by the states during the past 3-years will be disclosed.

A copy of the Employee NDR File Request Form is set forth at Appendix 34.

For general information on the National Driver Register, contact:

Highway Safety Programs
National Driver Register
400 7th Street SW., Washington, DC 20590-0001
Tel: (202) 366-4800
URL: http://www.nhtsa.dot.gov/people/perform/driver/

A directory of state National Driver Register contacts is set forth at Appendix 35.

CHAPTER 6:
FEDERAL LEGISLATION

IN GENERAL

As set forth below, Congress has established a number of Federal programs designed to encourage states to enact effective drunk driving laws and prevention programs. Oftentimes, Congress uses a "carrot and stick" approach to bringing states into compliance with its objectives.

INCENTIVE GRANTS UNDER THE TRANSPORTATION EQUITY ACT FOR THE 21ST CENTURY (TEA-21)

The Transportation Equity Act for the 21st Century (TEA-21) was signed into law by former President Clinton on June 9, 1998. Funding for TEA-21 was reauthorized on April 30, 2004, by passage of the Federal Highway Funding Under Surface Transportation Extension Act of 2004, Part II (P. L. 108-224). Section 5 of the Act extends funding for the two highway safety grant programs included in the legislation: (1) safety incentive grants for use of seat belts; and (2) safety incentives to prevent operation of motor vehicles by intoxicated persons. Section 5 also extended the National Highway Traffic Safety Administration (NHTSA) program.

Incentives to Prevent Operation of Motor Vehicles by Intoxicated Persons

TEA-21 provides funding for incentive grants to states that have enacted and are enforcing a law providing that any person with a blood alcohol concentration of 0.08 percent or greater while operating a motor vehicle in the state shall be deemed to have committed a per se offense of driving while intoxicated.

Alcohol-impaired Driving Countermeasures

TEA-21 makes basic grants to states that adopt and demonstrate specific programs, such as prompt suspension of the driver's license of an alcohol-impaired driver or graduated licensing systems for new drivers (Basic Grant A); or meet performance criteria showing reductions in fatalities involving impaired drivers (Basic Grant B). States receiving basic grants may be considered for up to six types of supplemental grants.

National Highway Traffic and Safety Administration Section 410 Program

The National Highway Traffic and Safety Administration (NHTSA) Section 410 program was originally established by Congress in 1988 and subsequently amended. Under the Section 410 program, states may qualify for basic and supplemental incentive grant funds by adopting and implementing comprehensive drunk driving prevention measures. To qualify for a grant under the 410 Program, a state is required to meet certain criteria.

Basic Grant Eligibility: Basic Grant A

A state is eligible for the Basic Grant A by adopting at least 5 of the following criteria:

1. Administrative License Revocation System—the establishment and maintenance of an expedited administrative license suspension or revocation system for impaired drivers who either fail or refuse to take a chemical test, which results in a 90-day suspension for first time offenders, and either a 1-year suspension or revocation for repeat offenders.

2. Underage Drinking Program (Under Age 21)—establishment and maintenance of an effective system for preventing individuals under age 21 from obtaining alcoholic beverages and for preventing persons from making alcoholic beverages available to individuals under age 21, including the issuance of "Under 21" driver's licenses that are tamper resistant or which are easily distinguishable in appearance from licenses issued to older drivers.

3. DWI Enforcement Program—establishment and maintenance of either (i) a statewide program for stopping motor vehicles on a nondiscriminatory lawful basis for determining whether the driver is impaired, or (ii) a statewide special traffic enforcement program for impaired driving that emphasizes publicity for the program.

4. Graduated Licensing System—establishment and maintenance of a 3-stage graduated licensing system for young drivers that includes nighttime driving restrictions during the first 2 stages, requires all vehicle occupants to be properly restrained, and makes it unlawful for a person under age 21 to operate a motor vehicle with a BAC of 0.02 percent or greater.

5. Program for Drivers with High BAC Levels—establishment and maintenance of a program to target individuals with high BAC levels who operate a motor vehicle, which may include implementation of a system of graduated penalties and assessment of individuals convicted of driving under the influence of alcohol.

6. Young Adult Drinking Program (Age 21-34)—establishment and maintenance of a program to reduce driving while under the influence of alcohol by individuals age 21 through 34, which may include awareness campaigns, traffic safety partnerships, assessment of first-time offenders, and incorporating treatment into sentencing.

7. BAC Testing System—establishment and maintenance of an effective system for increasing the rate of BAC testing of drivers involved in fatal accidents.

Basic Grant Eligibility: Basic Grant B

A state is eligible for the Basic Grant B by adopting the following criteria:

1. Fatal Impaired Driver Percentage Reduction—The state must demonstrate that the percentage of fatally injured drivers has decreased in each of the 3 most recent calendar years for which statistics for determining such percentages are available; and

2. Fatal Impaired Driver Percentage Comparison—The state must demonstrate that the percentage of fatally injured drivers has been lower than the average percentage for all states in each of the calendar years referred to above.

Supplemental Grants

Supplemental grants are available to states which meet 1 or more of the following criteria:

1. Video Equipment for Drunk Driver Detection Program—establishment and maintenance of a program to acquire video equipment to be used in detecting and prosecuting drivers operating under the influence of alcohol.

2. Self-Sustaining Drunk Driving Prevention Program—establishment and maintenance of a self-sustaining drunk driving prevention program under which a significant portion of the fines collected from individuals driving under the influence of alcohol are returned to those communities which have comprehensive DWI prevention programs.

3. Reduced Driving with Suspended License Law—establishment and maintenance of a law aimed at reducing the incidence of individuals driving with suspended license, which may require a "zebra"

stripe to be affixed and made clearly visible on the license plate of any motor vehicle owned and operated by a driver with a suspended license.

4. Use of Passive Alcohol Sensors—establishment and maintenance of a program to acquire passive alcohol sensors to be used by law enforcement officers in detecting drivers operating under the influence of alcohol.

5. Effective DWI Tracking System—establishment and maintenance of an effective DWI tracking system which may include data covering arrests, case prosecutions, court dispositions and sanctions.

6. Other Programs—establishment and maintenance of other innovative programs to reduce traffic safety problems resulting from individuals driving while under the influence of alcohol or controlled substances, including programs that seek to achieve a reduction through legal, judicial, enforcement, educational, technological, or other approaches.

THE IRS RESTRUCTURING BILL

In 1998, Congress passed legislation that requires states to (i) enact open container laws and (ii) provide for tougher penalties for repeat offenders. This legislation was originally supposed to be included in the Transportation Equity Act for the 21st Century (TEA-21), however, it was omitted due to a technical error. Thus, the new laws were attached to the IRS Restructuring Bill.

States that failed to comply with the legislation by October 1, 2003 were subject to having 1.5 percent of their federal highway construction funds redirected to traffic safety programs. Any funds transferred to the state's highway safety program may be used for alcohol-impaired driving countermeasures, or may be directed to state and local agencies for enforcement of related laws.

Open Container Laws

The legislation requires all states to enact an open container law which prohibits the possession or consumption of an open container of alcohol by the driver and all passengers in a motor vehicle. By 2004, forty-three states and the District of Columbia have laws prohibiting the driver, passengers or both from possessing an open container of alcohol in the passenger compartment of a vehicle.

A table of states with open container laws is set forth at Appendix 35.

Repeat Offender Legislation

Repeat offender legislation requires all states to establish stronger minimum penalties for repeat drunk-driving offenders, including: (i) a one-year minimum license suspension; (ii) vehicle impoundment provisions; (iii) vehicle immobilization or ignition interlock provisions; (iv) assessment and treatment of alcohol problems; and (v) mandatory jail time or community service for repeat offenders.

THE FEDERAL ZERO TOLERANCE PROGRAM

In November 1995, Congress established the Federal Zero Tolerance Program, which requires the withholding of certain Federal-aid highway funds from states that do not enact and enforce "zero tolerance" laws. To avoid withholding of funds, states were required to enact and enforce zero tolerance laws by October 1, 1998, that (i) set 0.02 percent BAC as the legal limit for all persons under the age of 21; (ii) make .0.2 percent BAC an "illegal per se" offense; and (iii) authorize license suspensions or revocations for any violation of the state zero tolerance law. As further set forth in Chapter 4, all states and the District of Columbia have since enacted zero tolerance laws.

PRESIDENTIAL DIRECTIVE—THE 0.08 BAC PERCENT INITIATIVE

On March 3, 1998, former President Clinton addressed representatives of national organizations, highway safety partners, and the nation, concerning proposed new federal standards to prevent impaired driving. The President called for a nationwide legal limit which would make it "illegal per se" to operate a motor vehicle at or above a BAC level of 0.08 percent across the country. The President directed the Secretary of Transportation to work with Congress, federal agencies, state governments, and other concerned groups to promote adoption of the limit. Since that time, legislation has been passed which lowered the BAC limit on federal lands, including national parks and Department of Defense installations, to 0.08%. In addition, numerous Native American tribes have also adopted the 0.08% BAC level on highways subject to their jurisdiction.

The National Minimum Drinking Age Act of 1984

In 1984, The National Minimum Drinking Age Act was enacted. The Act required all states to raise their minimum purchase and public possession of alcohol age to 21. States that did not comply faced a reduction in highway funds under the Federal Highway Aid Act. The U.S. Department of Transportation has determined that all states are in compliance with the Act. The Act was passed, in large part, to deter teenage drinking and driving in an effort to decrease teenage driving fatalities, as more fully discussed in Chapter 4 of this almanac.

The national law specifically requires states to prohibit purchase and public possession of alcoholic beverages. It does not require prohibition of persons under 21 from drinking alcoholic beverages. The term "public possession" is strictly defined and does not apply to possession of alcoholic beverages under the following circumstances:

1. An established religious purpose, when accompanied by a parent, spouse, or legal guardian age 21 or older;

2. Medical purposes when prescribed or administered by a licensed physician, pharmacist, dentist, nurse, hospital, or medical institution;

3. In private clubs or establishments; and

4. In the course of lawful employment by a duly licensed manufacturer, wholesaler or retailer.

CONGRESSIONAL STOP DUI CAUCUS

After Congress enacted legislation in the 1980s to uniformly raise the minimum drinking age to 21, and provide incentive grants to states that cracked down on drunk driving, states strengthened their laws, toughened their enforcement, and expanded their education campaigns. This nationwide action contributed to a 38 percent drop in alcohol-related traffic deaths from 1982 to 1994. DUI deaths then stagnated for five years before starting to climb again in 2000, 2001 and 2002.

With alcohol-related crashes on the rise after 20 years of decline, a bipartisan group of members of Congress announced the formation of the "Congressional Stop DUI Caucus." On May 19, 2004, Members of Congress, the National Commission Against Drunk Driving (NCADD), and the National Association of Broadcasters (NAB), launched the new Congressional STOP DUI Caucus at the Russell Senate Office Building in Washington, DC. The purpose of the STOP DUI Caucus is to work with states and local communities to help renew the nationwide war on drunk driving.

The Congressional Stop DUI Caucus is co-chaired by Reps. Jon Porter (R-NV), Shelley Berkley (D-NV) and Jim DeMint (R-SC). Other members to date are Senators Jeff Bingaman (D-NM), Michael DeWine (R-OH), Byron Dorgan (D-ND) and John Ensign (NV), and Reps. J. Gresham Barrett (SC), Henry Brown (R-SC), James Clyburn (D-SC), Elijah Cummings (D-MD), Trent Franks (R-AZ), Jim Gibbons (R-NV), Ron Kind (D-WI), James Oberstar (D-MN), Mike Oxley (R-OH), Frank Pallone

(D-NJ), Mike Rogers (R-MI), Dutch Ruppersberger (D-MD), John Spratt (D-SC), Tom Udall (NM), Chris Van Hollen (D-MD), Joe Wilson (R-SC) and Albert Wynn (D-MD).

THE NATIONAL COMMISSION AGAINST DRUNK DRIVING (NCADD)

The National Commission Against Drunk Driving (NCADD) is the successor to the Presidential Commission on Drunk Driving appointed by President Ronald Reagan in 1982. The Presidential Commission was given the task of finding solutions to the national epidemic of drunk driving. In the ten years following the Commission's final report to the nation, alcohol-related deaths dropped by more than 30%, and from 1982 to 1999, the number of traffic fatalities involving alcohol decreased 36.5% from 25,165 to 15,976.

The mission of the National Commission Against Drunk Driving is to continue the efforts of the Presidential Commission On Drunk Driving to reduce impaired driving by uniting a broad based coalition of public and private sector organizations and other concerned individuals. The Commission works closely with all related federal, state, and local officials, as well as interested private sector groups, to identify and develop strategies and programs that will reduce impaired driving. The Commission can be reached at the following address:

National Commission Against Drunk Driving (NCADD)
8403 Colesville Road, Suite 370
Silver Spring, MD 20910
Phone: 240-247-6004
Fax: 240-247-7012
E-mail: info@ncadd.com

CHAPTER 7:
VICTIMS RIGHTS

IN GENERAL

When a family member is murdered, the survivors' only recourse is to the criminal justice system to bring the criminal to justice, and thus provide the family with some closure to the tragedy. Historically, family members were not generally viewed as "victims of the crime," and they had little or no official involvement in the proceedings.

In recent years, this has begun to change, in large part due to the activism of the victims' rights movement. A victims rights movement has emerged over the past two decades to champion the rights of crime victims, including those victimized by the acts of drunk drivers. The victims' rights movement has fought to have the family of a homicide victim recognized as victims of the crime who are entitled to actively participate in the criminal proceedings. This movement has been responsible for the passage of important federal, state and local legislation that provide victims with certain rights and allow them to be active participants in the criminal justice process.

A common feature of many of these laws—sometimes referred to as a "Victims' Bill of Rights"—is the opportunity of victims to make their wishes known at the time of sentencing. This is known as a "victim impact statement," as further discussed below. Other statutory rights that may be provided to crime victims, witnesses to a crime, and the family members of a homicide victim include:

1. The right to attend the criminal proceedings, including the trial, the sentencing, and any subsequent parole hearings, and the right to be heard;

2. The right to be notified of each stage of the criminal proceedings so that the victim can participate if he or she wishes to do so.

3. The right to compensation—such as that provided by state victim compensation programs—and restitution by the offender, including the right to recover compensation derived from the criminal's exploitation of the crime;

4. The right to be informed of all available legal remedies, including the right to pursue civil action against the criminal, e.g. to recover punitive damages; and

5. The right to be protected from harassment, including security during the criminal proceedings, and relocation assistance if warranted;

6. The right to have the opportunity to inform the court of the impact of the crime and to request the court to submit such information to the parole board for inclusion in its records.

Under Section 11-1502 of the Uniform Vehicle Code, victims of a traffic-related offense are guaranteed the following rights:

Section 11-1502. Rights of Victims. Victims shall have the following rights:

(a) To speedy prosecution of the offense. In any criminal justice proceeding, the police, the prosecutor, and the court shall take appropriate action to ensure speedy prosecution of the defendant. Victims shall be informed by the prosecuting attorney of any motions which would result in delay of the prosecution and be allowed to object in writing.

(b) Upon request by the victim, to be informed by the police investigating the case of the status of the investigation, and by the prosecuting attorney prior to any critical decisions concerning the case including the charging decision, diversion, dismissal, or other disposition.

(c) To be present at any time the defendant has the right to be present during all criminal justice proceedings related to an offense unless the court determines that exclusion is necessary to protect the confidentiality of juvenile or similar proceedings. If a victim is unable to attend the court proceedings, the court may designate a representative of the victim who has the same right to be present as the victim would have had.

(d) To make victim impact statements to the court including information about the financial, emotional, psychological, and physical effects of the crime on the victim, the circumstances surrounding the crime, the manner in which it was perpetrated, and the victim's opinion of any recommended sentence of the convicted offender. A victim may present an impact statement to the court either orally or in writing.

(e) To an order of restitution if the order is authorized by the laws of this state.

As set forth in Appendix 15, the Uniform Vehicle Code also details the responsibilities incumbent upon the law enforcement agency and the prosecutor's office to provide victims of traffic-related offenses with resource information concerning support groups and the availability of services, and details about the criminal proceedings.

THE VICTIM IMPACT STATEMENT

A *victim impact statement* is a written or oral report which details the manner in which the crime affected the victim and the victim's family. The statement is commonly given at the time of sentencing, and at parole hearings at the time the criminal becomes eligible for parole. The victim impact statement is usually offered by the victim, or the victim's survivors. In the case of a minor or incompetent victim, the statement may be offered by the parents or legal guardian of the victim.

The victim impact statement brings to the court's attention the pain and suffering caused by the crime, which may be expected to endure long after the criminal is sentenced. For example, the statement may describe the physical, mental or financial harm the crime has caused the family. The victim impact statement also gives the victim and/or the victim's family, the chance to participate more fully in the criminal justice process and the quest to bring the criminal to justice. Many states even allow the victim to recommend a sentence or offer comments on the proposed sentence.

Most states have laws which give the victim and/or the victim's family, the right to make a victim impact statement, and require the court or the parole board to consider the statement when rendering a decision. The statement may also be contained in the criminal's presentencing report to the court, and periodically updated and sent to the parole board.

Under Section 11-505 of the Uniform Vehicle Code, the Probation Department must include a written victim impact statement as part of the pre-sentence report if the victim chooses to submit one:

> Section 11-1505. Probation Department. The Probation Department, in preparing any pre-sentence report on the defendant, must attempt to consult with the victim and must include a written victim impact statement as part of the pre-sentence report if the victim

chooses to submit one. If the victim cannot be located or declines to cooperate, the probation officer must include a notation to that effect in the report.

In addition, Section 11-1506 of the Uniform Vehicle Code provides that the Court must orally inform victims present at the sentencing hearing of their right to present victim impact statements.

RESTITUTION

Restitution is money that the Court orders the defendant to pay the victim to compensate them for their expenses resulting from the crime, such as medical expenses, lost wages, etc.. Restitution is a part of the defendant's sentence. Generally, the defendant's probation officer is responsible for making sure that a payment schedule is set up and that payments are made to the victim. If the victim does not receive the scheduled payments, they may contact the defendant's probation officer. If the offender has not paid restitution according to the judge or probation officer's guidelines, victims have the right to request a probation review hearing. The probation officer can request a hearing at any time, and must ask for a hearing if the restitution has not been paid 60 days prior to the end of the offender's probation. If the offender has been released from prison, they can also be held responsible for payment during their supervised release period. If payment does not occur during this period, the offender can be sent to prison for the remainder of the sentence.

If the defendant does not voluntarily pay the court-ordered restitution, in order to collect the money, the victim may have to initiate collection proceedings by obtaining a judgment or writ of execution from the Court. The local sheriff executes order by seizing property belonging to the defendant. In addition, most states have some type of crime victims reparations program which provides financial assistance to victims of violent crimes.

VICTIM ASSISTANCE ORGANIZATIONS

Crime victims often do not know where to turn for help in dealing with the emotional aftermath of the crime. Many local communities offer programs to assist the victim. Such programs are usually listed in the telephone directory under "victim's assistance." In addition, assistance may be found by contacting local social services or mental health organizations.

Most victims assistance organizations provide a wide variety of programs, including therapy and counseling; support groups; and practical help and information. For example, assistance may be provided in obtaining compensation from state victim compensation boards, or in completing a victim impact statement.

As further discussed below, one of the strongest advocates for those victimized by drunk drivers is Mothers Against Drunk Driving (MADD).

Mothers Against Drunk Driving (MADD)

Mothers Against Drunk Driving (MADD) is a non-profit grassroots organization begun by Cyndi Lightner, after her 13-year-old daughter, Cari, was killed by a hit-and-run drunk driver. The driver was a repeat offender and, prior to Cari's death, had been out of jail on bail for only two days after having caused another hit-and-run drunk driving crash. The driver also had three previous drunk driving arrests and two convictions. Cari's mother decided to take action so other families would not have to suffer the same tragedy.

MADD's stated mission is to look for effective solutions to drunk driving and underage drinking problems, and to assist victims of violent drunk driving crimes. MADD has been particularly effective in lobbying for victims' rights, and has initiated actions to bring about tougher laws against impaired driving, to provide for stiffer penalties for such crimes, and to increase public greater awareness on the perils of driving drunk.

Since its founding in 1980, MADD has helped pass more than 2,300 anti-drunk driving laws across the country. MADD has continued to grow and pursue the efforts initiated by its founder, and has approximately 600 chapters nationwide. MADD now has nearly three million members and supporters nationwide and abroad, making it the largest victim-advocate and anti-DWI activist organization in the USA and the world.

Along with its rapid growth, MADD recognized the need for more professional, trained management and administration and a more sophisticated approach to communications and dealing with the media, as well as training in DWI issues, the legislative process and victim assistance. Coordination to meet these needs is handled by a national headquarters staff of approximately 60 individuals who direct training opportunities, seasonal and ongoing education and awareness programs, national fundraising, media campaigns, and federal and state legislative activities.

Regular monthly or bimonthly mailings of program materials and other timely information from the National Office further reinforce the direction of the organization. Special training opportunities are held, including victim assistance institutes and impaired driving issues workshops, which may also include other pertinent state and community leaders outside of MADD. For more information, readers may contact MADD Headquarters at P.O. Box 541688, Dallas, TX 75354-1688 or visit their website at http://www.madd.org.

APPENDIX 1:
DIRECTORY OF NHTSA REGIONAL OFFICES

REGION	ADDRESS	TELEPHONE	FACSIMILE	EMAIL	AREAS COVERED
NHTSA Region 1—New England	Transportation Systems Center 55 Broadway Kendall Square—Code 903 Cambridge, MA 02142	617-494-3427	617-494-3646	region1@nhtsa.dot.gov	CT, ME, MA, NH, RI, VT
NHTSA Region 2—Eastern Region	222 Mamaroneck Avenue, Suite 204 White Plains, NY 10605	914-682-6162	914-682-6239	region2@nhtsa.dot.gov	NY, NJ, PR, VI
NHTSA Region 3—Mid Atlantic Region	10 South Howard Street Suite 6700 Baltimore, MD 21201	410-962-0090	410-962-2770	region3@nhtsa.dot.gov	DE, DC, MD, PA, VA, WV
NHTSA Region 4—Southeast Region	61 Forsyth Street SW Atlanta, GA 30303	404-562-3739	404-562-3763	region4@nhtsa.dot.gov	AL, FL, GA, KY, MS, NC, SC, TN

REGION	ADDRESS	TELEPHONE	FACSIMILE	EMAIL	AREAS COVERED
NHTSA Region 5—Great Lakes Region	19900 Governors Drive Suite 201 Olympia Fields, IL 60461	708-503-8822	708-503-8991	region5@nhtsa.dot.gov	IL, IN, MI, MN, OH, WI
NHTSA Region 6—South Central Region	819 Taylor Street Room 8a38 Fort Worth, TX 76102	817-978-3653	817-978-8339	region6@nhtsa.dot.gov	AR, LA, NM, OK, TX, Indian Nations
NHTSA Region 7—Central Region	901 Locust Street Room 466 Kansas City, MO 64106	816-329-3900	816-329-3910	region7@nhtsa.dot.gov	IA, KS, MO, NE
NHTSA Region 8—Rocky Mountain Region	555 Zang Street Room 430 Lakewood, CO 80228	303-969-6917	303-969-6294	region8@nhtsa.dot.gov	CO, MT, ND, SD, UT, WY
NHTSA Region 9—Western Region	201 Mission Street Suite 2230 San Francisco, CA 94105	415-744-3089	415-744-2532	region9@nhtsa.dot.gov	AZ, CA, HI, NV, American Samoa, Guam, Mariana Islands
NHTSA Region 10—Northwest Region	3140 Jackson Federal Building 915 Second Avenue Seattle, WA 98174	206-220-7640	206-220-7651	region10@nhtsa.dot.gov	AK, ID, OR, WA

Source: National Highway Transportation Safety Administration.

APPENDIX 2:
TYPES OF FATALITIES IN CRASHES INVOLVING AT LEAST ONE INTOXICATED DRIVER OR NONOCCUPANT IN 2002

TYPE OF FATALITY	NUMBER	PERCENT OF TOTAL
Intoxicated Drivers	8,474	56
Nonintoxicated Drivers	1,054	7
Passengers	3,219	21
Intoxicated Nonoccupants (Pedestrians and Pedalcyclists)	1,761	12
Nonintoxicated Nonoccupants	511	3
Total Fatalities	15,019	100

Source: National Highway Transportation Safety Administration.

APPENDIX 3:
NUMBER OF TRAFFIC FATALITIES BY
STATE AND BAC LEVEL—2002

STATE	TOTAL TRAFFIC FATALITIES	BAC LEVEL 0.00	BAC LEVEL 0.01-0.07	BAC LEVEL 0.08 OR GREATER
ALABAMA	1033	620	43	370
ALASKA	87	52	2	34
ARIZONA	1117	640	58	420
ARKANSAS	640	398	35	207
CALIFORNIA	4078	2466	300	1312
COLORADO	742	435	39	268
CONNECTICUT	322	182	17	123
DELAWARE	124	73	8	43
DISTRICT OF COLUMBIA	47	22	3	22
FLORIDA	3132	1856	177	1099
GEORGIA,	1523	994	90	439
HAWAII	119	69	10	41
IDAHO	264	173	17	74
ILLINOIS	1411	763	97	552
INDIANA	792	523	46	223
IOWA	404	273	24	107
KANSAS	512	283	23	205
KENTUCKY	915	614	39	263
LOUISIANA	875	462	62	351
MAINE	216	165	4	47
MARYLAND	659	394	49	216
MASSACHUSETTS	459	238	30	192

STATE	TOTAL TRAFFIC FATALITIES	BAC LEVEL 0.00	BAC LEVEL 0.01-0.07	BAC LEVEL 0.08 OR GREATER
MICHIGAN	1277	787	68	422
MINNESOTA	657	402	46	209
MISSISSIPPI	885	553	41	292
MISSOURI	1208	683	68	457
MONTANA	270	143	21	106
NEBRASKA	307	190	21	97
NEVADA	381	210	23	148
NEW HAMPSHIRE	127	76	5	46
NEW JERSEY	773	474	45	254
NEW MEXICO	449	234	27	189
NEW YORK	1522	1044	77	400
NORTH CAROLINA	1575	974	67	533
NORTH DAKOTA	97	49	8	40
OHIO	1418	856	66	496
OKLAHOMA	734	485	35	215
OREGON	436	257	26	153
PENNSYLVANIA	1614	958	88	568
RHODE ISLAND	84	38	8	38
SOUTH CAROLINA	1053	502	64	487
SOUTH DAKOTA	180	88	13	80
TENNESSEE	1175	704	61	410
TEXAS	3725	1980	194	1551
UTAH	328	255	7	67
VERMONT	78	51	5	22
VIRGINIA	914	544	48	323
WASHINGTON	659	361	32	265
WEST VIRGINIA	439	259	20	160
WISCONSIN	803	440	39	325
WYOMING	176	107	7	62
U.S. TOTAL	42,815	25,396	2,401	15,019

Source: National Highway Transportation Safety Administration.

APPENDIX 4:
NUMBER OF DRIVER FATALITIES IN 2002, BY TIME OF DAY AND BAC LEVEL

TIME OF DAY	NUMBER OF DRIVERS INVOLVED IN FATAL CRASHES	PERCENTAGE WITH BAC LEVEL OF 0.08 OR GREATER
Daytime—6AM-6PM	13,538	13%
Nighttime—6PM-6AM	12,745	52%

Source: National Highway Transportation Safety Administration.

APPENDIX 5:
NUMBER OF DRIVER FATALITIES IN 2002, BY DAY OF WEEK AND BAC LEVEL

DAY OF WEEK	NUMBER OF DRIVERS IN-VOLVED IN FATAL CRASHES	PERCENTAGE WITH BAC LEVEL OF 0.08 OR GREATER
Weekday—Monday 6AM—Friday 6PM	15,772	24%
Weeknight—Friday 6PM—Monday 6AM	10,714	44%

Source: National Highway Transportation Safety Administration.

APPENDIX 6:
NUMBER OF DRIVERS INVOLVED IN FATAL CRASHES IN 2002 BY AGE AND BAC LEVEL

AGE	NUMBER OF DRIVERS IN-VOLVED IN FATAL CRASHES	PERCENTAGE WITH BAC LEVEL OF 0.08 OR GREATER
16-20	8,082	17%
21-24	6,285	33%
25-34	11,416	28%
35-44	10,896	26%
45-64	13,580	17%
Over 64	6,271	5%

Source: National Highway Transportation Safety Administration.

APPENDIX 7:
NUMBER OF DRIVERS INVOLVED IN FATAL CRASHES IN 2002, BY GENDER AND BAC LEVEL

GENDER	NUMBER OF DRIVERS INVOLVED	NO ALCOHOL (0.00)	0.01-0.07	0.08 AND GREATER
Male	29,629	71%	5%	24%
Female	14,867	84%	3%	13%
Total	57,480	74%	4%	21%

Source: National Highway Transportation Safety Administration.

APPENDIX 8:
NUMBER OF DRIVERS INVOLVED IN FATAL CRASHES IN 2002, BY VEHICLE TYPE AND BAC LEVEL

VEHICLE TYPE	NUMBER OF DRIVERS INVOLVED IN FATAL CRASHES	PERCENTAGE WITH BAC LEVEL OF 0.08 OR GREATER
Passenger Car	26,966	22%
Light Truck	21,373	23%
Large Truck	4,508	2%
Motorcycle	3,337	31%

Source: National Highway Transportation Safety Administration.

APPENDIX 9:
NUMBER OF DRIVERS INVOLVED IN FATAL CRASHES IN 2002, BY SAFETY BELT USE AND BAC LEVEL

SAFETY BELT USE	NUMBER OF DRIVERS INVOLVED	NO ALCOHOL (0.00)	0.01-0.07	0.08 AND GREATER
Used	27,068	85%	3%	12%
Not Used	16,455	54%	6%	40%
Total	47,882	73%	4%	23%

Source: National Highway Transportation Safety Administration.

APPENDIX 10:
NUMBER OF DRIVERS INVOLVED IN FATAL CRASHES IN 2002, BY INJURY SEVERITY AND BAC LEVEL

INJURY SEVERITY	NUMBER OF DRIVERS INVOLVED	NO ALCOHOL (0.00)	0.01-0.07	0.08 AND GREATER
Fatal	25,840	63%	5%	32%
Survived	31,640	84%	4%	13%
Total	57,480	74%	4%	21%

Source: National Highway Transportation Safety Administration.

APPENDIX 11:
EXTENT OF INTOXICATION AMONG DRIVERS INVOLVED IN FATAL CRASHES BY PRIOR CONVICTIONS OF THE DRIVER (1997-2001)

YEAR	NO PRIOR DWI CONVICTIONS	PRIOR DWI CONVICTIONS
1997	19%	63%
1998	19%	61%
1999	19%	63%
2000	20%	63%
2001	20%	62%

Source: National Highway Transportation Safety Administration.

APPENDIX 12:
PREVIOUS DRIVING RECORDS OF DRIVERS KILLED IN TRAFFIC CRASHES IN 2002, BY BLOOD ALCOHOL CONCENTRATION (BAC) LEVEL

BAC LEVEL	RECORDED CRASHES	DWI CONVICTIONS	SPEEDING CONVICTIONS	RECORDED SUSPENSIONS OR REVOCATIONS
BAC 0.00	15%	2%	19%	9%
BAC 0.01-0.07	16%	5%	25%	22%
BAC 0.08 or greater	17%	10%	24%	24%

Source: National Highway Transportation Safety Administration.

APPENDIX 13:
NUMBER OF PEDESTRIANS KILLED IN FATAL CRASHES IN 2002, BY AGE AND BAC LEVEL

AGE	NUMBER OF PEDESTRIAN FATALITIES	PERCENTAGE WITH BAC LEVEL OF 0.08 OR GREATER
16-20	283	31%
21-24	243	49%
25-34	597	48%
35-44	851	53%
45-64	1,291	40%
Over 64	1,051	10%

Source: National Highway Transportation Safety Administration.

APPENDIX 14:
NUMBER OF DRIVERS INVOLVED IN FATAL CRASHES IN 2002, BY TYPE OF CRASH AND BAC LEVEL

TYPE OF CRASH	NUMBER OF DRIVERS INVOLVED	NO ALCOHOL (0.00)	0.01-0.07	0.08 AND GREATER
Single Vehicle Crash	21,365	57%	6%	37%
Multiple Vehicle Crash	36,115	85%	3%	12%
Total	57,480	74%	4%	21%

Source: National Highway Transportation Safety Administration.

APPENDIX 15:
SELECTED PROVISIONS OF THE UNIFORM VEHICLE CODE RELATED TO DRUNK DRIVING

CHAPTER 6—ARTICLE I—ISSUANCE OF LICENSES, EXPIRATION AND RENEWAL

SECTION 6-103. Persons not to be licensed.

(b) Ineligibility. The department shall not issue any driver's license to, nor renew the driver's license of, any person:

1. Who is an habitual user of alcohol or any drug to a degree rendering such person incapable of safely driving a motor vehicle.

CHAPTER 6—ARTICLE II—CANCELLATION, SUSPENSION, OR REVOCATION OF LICENSES

SECTION 6-206. Mandatory revocation of license by department.

The department shall forthwith revoke the license of any driver upon receiving a record of such driver's conviction of any of the following offenses:

1. Homicide by vehicle (or manslaughter resulting from the operation of a motor vehicle;

2. Driving or being in actual physical control of a motor vehicle while under the influence of alcohol or any drug as prohibited by §11-902;

3. Any felony in the commission of which a motor vehicle is used;

4. Failure to stop, render aid or identify the driver as required by §10-102 in the event of a motor vehicle accident resulting in the death or personal injury of another;

5. Perjury or the making of a false affidavit or statement under oath to the department under this code or under any other law relating to the ownership or operation of motor vehicles.

6. Unauthorized use of a motor vehicle belonging to another which act does not amount to a felony;

7. The unlawful use of a license as prohibited by §6-301(a).

SECTION 6-207. Revocation of license for refusal to submit to a chemical test or having BAC of 0.08 or more.

(a) Any person who operates a motor vehicle upon the highways of this State shall be deemed to have given consent, subject to the provisions of §11-903, to a test or tests of such operator's blood, breath, or urine for the purpose of determining operator's alcohol concentration or the presence of other drugs. The test or tests shall be administered at the direction of a law enforcement officer who has probable cause to believe the person has been violating §11-902(a), and one of the following conditions exists:

1. The person has been arrested for violating §11-902(a) or any other offense alleged to have been committed while the person was violating §11-902(a);

2. The person has been involved in an accident;

3. The person has refused to submit to the preliminary screening test authorized by §6-209; or

4. The person has submitted to the preliminary screening test authorized by §6-209 which disclosed an alcohol concentration of 0.08 or more.

The law enforcement agency by which such officer is employed shall designate which of the aforesaid tests shall be administered.

(b) Any person who is dead, unconscious or who is otherwise in a condition rendering one incapable of refusal, shall be deemed not to have withdrawn the consent provided by paragraph (a) of this section and the test or tests may be administered, subject to the provisions of §11-903.

(c) A person requested to submit to a test as provided above shall be warned by the law enforcement officer requesting the test that a refusal to submit to the test will result in revocation of such person's license to operate a motor vehicle for (six months) (one year). Following this warning, if a person under arrest refuses upon the request of a law enforcement officer to submit to a test designated by the law enforcement agency as provided in paragraph (a) of this section, none shall be given.

(d) If the person refuses testing or submits to a test which discloses an alcohol concentration of 0.08 or more under this section, the law enforcement officer shall submit a sworn report to the department, certifying that the test was requested pursuant to subsection (a) and that the person refused to submit to testing or submitted to a test which disclosed an alcohol concentration of 0.08 or more.

(e) Upon receipt of the sworn report of a law enforcement officer submitted under subsection (d), the department shall revoke the driver's license of the person for the periods specified in §6-214.

(f) On behalf of the department, the law enforcement officer submitting the sworn report under subsection (d) shall serve immediate notice of the revocation on the person, and the revocation shall be effective (7) (10) (15) days after the date of service. If the person has a valid license, the officer shall take the driver's license of the person, and issue a temporary license valid for the notice period. The officer shall send the license to the department along with the sworn report under subsection (d).

In cases where no notice has been served by the law enforcement officer, the department shall give notice as provided in §2-314 and the revocation shall be effective (7) (10) (15) days after the date of service. If the address shown in the law enforcement officer's report differs from that shown on the department records, the notice shall be mailed to both addresses.

SECTION 6-208. Revocation of license for refusal to submit to chemical test or having BAC of any measurable and detectable amount for person under age (21).

(a) The phrase "any measurable and detectable amount of alcohol" shall be defined as the alcohol concentration in a person's blood or breath which is 0.02 or more based on the definition of blood and breath units as defined in §11-903(a)(5).

(b) Any person under age (21) who drives or is in actual physical control of any vehicle upon the highways of this State shall be deemed to have given consent, subject to the provisions of §11-903, to a test or tests of such person's blood, breath, or urine for the purpose of determining such person's alcohol concentration or the presence of other drugs. The test or tests shall be administered at the direction of a law enforcement officer who has probable cause to believe the person has been violating §11-902 (a), and one of the following conditions exists:

1. The person under age (21) has been arrested for violating §11-902 (a) or any other offense alleged to have been committed while the person was violating §11-902 (a);

2. The person under age (21) has been involved in an accident;

3. The person under age (21) has refused to submit to the preliminary screening test authorized by §6-209; or

4. The person under age (21) has submitted to the preliminary screening test authorized by §6-209; which disclosed an alcohol concentration of any measurable and detectable amount.

The law enforcement agency by which such officer is employed shall designate which of the aforesaid tests shall be administered.

(c) Any person under age (2l) who is dead, unconscious or who is otherwise in a condition rendering such person incapable of refusal, shall be deemed not to have withdrawn the consent provided by paragraph (b) of this section and the test or tests may be administered, subject to the provisions of §11-903.

(d) A person under age (21) requested to submit to a test as provided above shall be warned by the law enforcement officer requesting the test that a refusal to submit to the test will result in revocation of such person's license to operate a vehicle for (six months) (one year). Following this warning, if a person under arrest refuses upon the request of a law enforcement officer to submit to a test designated by the law enforcement agency as provided in paragraph (b) of this section, none shall be given.

(e) If the person under the age (2l) refuses testing or submits to a test which discloses an alcohol concentration of any measurable and detectable amount under this section, the law enforcement officer shall submit a sworn report to the department, certifying that the test was requested pursuant to subsection (b) and that the person refused to submit to testing or submitted to a test which disclosed an alcohol concentration of any measurable and detectable amount.

(f) Upon receipt of the sworn report of a law enforcement officer submitted under subsection (e), the department shall revoke the driver's license of the person for the periods specified in §6-214.

(g) On behalf of the department, the law enforcement officer submitting the sworn report under subsection (e) shall serve immediate notice of the revocation on the person, and the revocation shall be effective (7) (10) (15) days after the date of service. If the person has a valid license, the officer shall take the driver's license of the person, and issue a temporary license valid for the notice period. The officer shall send the license to the department along with the sworn report under subsection (e).

In cases where no notice has been served by the law enforcement officer, the department shall give notice as provided in §2-314 and the revocation shall be effective (7) (10) (15) days after the date of service. If the address shown in the law enforcement officer's report differs from that shown on the department records, the notice shall be mailed to both addresses.

SECTION 6-209. Preliminary breath test.

When a law enforcement officer has articulable grounds to suspect that a person may have been violating §11-902(a), the officer may request the suspect to submit to a preliminary screening test of suspect's breath to determine such person's alcohol concentration using a device approved by the (State Department of Health) for that purpose. In addition to this test, or upon a refusal to submit to testing, the officer may require further testing under §6-207.

SECTION 6-210. Chemical test of drivers in serious personal injury or fatal crashes.

Notwithstanding the provision's of §6-207, when the driver of a vehicle is involved in an accident resulting in death or serious personal injury of another person, and there is reason to believe that the driver is guilty of a violation of §11-902(a), the driver may be compelled by a police officer to submit to a test or tests of driver's blood, breath, or urine to determine the alcohol concentration or the presence of other drugs.

SECTION 6-211. Authority of department to suspend or revoke license.

(a) The department is hereby authorized to suspend the license of a driver upon a showing by its records or other sufficient evidence that the licensee:

1. Has committed an offense for which mandatory revocation of license is required upon conviction;

2. Has been convicted with such frequency of serious offenses against traffic regulations governing the movement of vehicles as to indicate a disrespect for traffic laws and a disregard for the safety of other persons on the highways;

3. Is an habitually reckless or negligent driver of a motor vehicle, such fact being established by the point system in subsection (b), by a record of accidents, or by other evidence;

4. Is incompetent to drive a motor vehicle;

5. Has permitted an unlawful or fraudulent use of such license;

6. Has violated driver's written promise to appear given to an officer upon the issuance of a traffic citation in this or any other state or has failed to appear in court in this or any other state at the time specified by the court;

7. Has been convicted of fleeing or attempting to elude a police officer; or

8. Has been convicted of racing on the highways.

9. Has failed to comply with the compulsory insurance or financial responsibility requirements of Chapter 7, where license suspension is specifically authorized under that chapter.

(b) For the purpose of identifying habitually reckless or negligent drivers and habitual or frequent violators of traffic regulations governing the movement of vehicles, the department shall adopt regulations establishing a uniform system assigning demerit points for convictions of violations of Chapter 11 of this code or of ordinances adopted by local authorities regulating the operation of motor vehicles. The regulations shall include a designated level of point accumulation which so identifies drivers. The department may assess points for convictions in other states of offenses which, if committed in this State, would be grounds for such assessment. Notice of each assessment of points may be given, but notice is required when the point accumulation reaches (xx) percent of the number at which suspension is authorized. No points shall be assessed for violating a provision of this code or municipal ordinance regulating standing, parking, equipment, size or weight. The department is authorized to suspend the license of a driver when such person's driving record identifies driver as an habitually reckless or negligent driver or as an habitual or frequent violator under this subsection. The department may, in accordance with its rules and regulations, order the licensee to attend a group or private driver improvement interview regarding such person's driving ability and record.

SECTION 6-212. Opportunity for hearing required.

(a) A suspension or revocation of a license under §6-114, 6-211, or 10-109 shall not become effective until the person is notified in writing and given an opportunity for a hearing.

1. The hearing shall be held within 20 days after receipt of a request for a hearing in the county where the alleged offense occurred unless the department and the licensee agree to a hearing in some other county. A record of all hearings shall be made.

2. Upon such hearing, the department shall rescind its order of revocation or suspension or, good cause appearing therefor, may modify or reaffirm its order.

2. Upon such hearing, the department shall rescind its order of revocation or suspension or, good cause appearing therefor, may modify or reaffirm its order.

(b) A revocation of license under Section §-207 shall become effective (7) (10) (15) days after the date of service of the notice of revocation.

1. At any time prior to the hearing provided in subsection (b)2, the person may request in writing an administrative review of the order of revocation. Upon receiving the request the department shall review the order, the evidence upon which it is based, including whether the person was driving or in actual physical control of a motor vehicle, and any other material information brought to the attention of the department, and determine whether sufficient cause exists to sustain the order. Within 15 days of receiving the request, the department shall report in writing the results of the review. The availability of the administrative review of the order shall have no effect upon the availability of judicial review as provided in §6-219.

2. Any person whose license is revoked under §6-207 may request a hearing in writing. The request shall state the grounds upon which the person seeks to have the revocation rescinded. The filing of the request shall not stay the revocation. The hearing shall be held within 20 days after filing of the request in the county in which the alleged offense occurred, unless the person and the department agree to a different location. The hearing shall be recorded, and be conducted by the department's designated agent. The hearing may be conducted upon a review of the law enforcement officer's own reports; provided, however, that the person may subpoena the officer. The department may issue subpoenas to compel the attendance of witnesses.

The scope of the hearing shall be limited to the issues of:

(1) Whether the law enforcement officer requested the test pursuant to §6-207;

(2) Whether the person was warned as required by §6-207(c);

(3) Whether the person was driving or in actual physical control of a motor vehicle;

(4) Whether the person refused to submit to the testing as provided in §6-207; or

(5) Whether a properly administered test or tests disclosed an alcohol concentration of 0.08 or more.

SECTION 6-214. Period of revocation.

(a) Unless the revocation was for a cause which has been removed, any person whose license or privilege to drive a motor vehicle on the public highways has been revoked shall not be eligible to apply for a new license nor restoration of such person's nonresident operating privilege until the expiration of:

1. (Six months) (One year) from the date on which the revoked license was surrendered to and received by the department or from such other date as shall be determined by the department in cases of revocation for; refusal to submit to a chemical test under the provisions of §6-207. (REVISED, 1984.)

2. (Three months) (Six months) from the date on which the revoked license was surrendered to and received by the department or from such other date as shall be determined by the department in cases of revocation for submitting to a test disclosing an alcohol concentration of 0.08 or more under the provisions of §6-207.

3. One year from the date on which the license was surrendered to a court under §6-205.

4. One year from the date on which the revoked license was surrendered to and received by the department.

5. Or, in all other revocation cases, one year commencing on a date determined by the department.

(b) Following a license revocation under §6-206(2) or 6-207, the department shall not issue a new license or otherwise restore the driving privilege unless and until the person presents evidence satisfactory to the department that it will be reasonably safe to permit the person to drive a motor vehicle upon the highways. No driving privilege may be restored until all applicable reinstatement fees have been paid.

(c) Except for revocations under §6-206(2) and 6-207, the department shall not issue a new license nor restore a person's revoked nonresident operating privilege unless and until it is satisfied after investigation of the character, habits and driving ability of such person that it will be safe to grant the privilege of driving a motor vehicle on the highways.

(d) Where a license or driving privilege has been revoked under §6-207 and the person is also convicted on criminal charges arising out of the same event for a violation of an offense under §11-902(a), and a revocation has been imposed under §6-206(2), both revocations shall be imposed but the total period of revocation shall not exceed the longer of the two revocation periods.

SECTION 6-215. Limited license.

Notwithstanding §6-214 and 6-303, following a license revocation under §6-206(2) or 6-207, the department may issue after 30 days a limited license to the driver if no prior limited license has been issued within the preceding 12 months and there have been no other such prior revocations. The department in issuing a limited license may impose the conditions and limitations which in its judgment are necessary to the interests of the public safety and welfare. The license may be limited to the operation of particular vehicles and to particular classes and time of operation. The limited license issued by the department shall clearly indicate the limitations imposed and the driver operating under a limited license shall have the license in driver's possession at all times when operating as a driver.

SECTION 6-216. Period of suspension.

(a) The department shall not suspend a driver's license or privilege to drive a motor vehicle on the public highways for a period of more than one year, except as permitted under §6-303 or under Chapter 7.

(b) At the end of the period of suspension a license surrendered to the department under §6-217 shall be returned to the licensee.

SECTION 6-217. Surrender and return of license; duty of officers.

(a) The department upon canceling, suspending or revoking a license shall require that such license shall be surrendered to and be retained by the department.

(b) Any person whose license has been canceled, suspended or revoked shall immediately return the license to the department.

(c) A law enforcement officer who in the course of duty encounters any canceled, suspended, or revoked drivers license shall seize and return such license to the department immediately.

6-218. No operation under foreign license during suspension or revocation in this State.

Any resident or nonresident whose driver's license or privilege to operate a motor vehicle in this State has been suspended or revoked as provided in this code shall not operate a motor vehicle in this State under a license or permit issued by any other jurisdiction or otherwise during such suspension or after such revocation until a new license is obtained when and as permitted under this chapter.

SECTION 6-219. Right of appeal to court.

(a) Any person denied a license or whose license has been canceled or revoked by the department, except where such cancellation or revocation is mandatory under the provisions of this code, and except any person whose license has been revoked under §6-207 shall have the right to file a petition within 30 days thereafter for a hearing in the matter in (a court of record) in the county wherein such person shall reside, or in the case of a nonresident's operating privilege in the county in which the main office of the department is located, and such court is hereby vested with jurisdiction and it shall be its duty to set the matter for hearing upon 30 days' written notice to the department, and thereupon to take testimony and examine into the facts of the case and to determine whether the petitioner is entitled to a license or is subject to denial, cancellation or revocation of license under the provisions of this chapter.

(b) Any person whose driving privileges have been revoked under the provisions of §6-207, may petition the (court of record) in the county in which such person resides for review of the decision on administrative review conducted under §6-212. The petition for review shall state the factual and legal claims upon which the petitioner relies, and shall be filed within (15) (30) days after notice of the decision on administrative review, together with proof of service of a copy thereof upon the department. The court shall set the matter for review upon thirty days' written notice to the department upon receipt of the record. The review shall be on the record, without taking additional testimony. If the court finds that the department exceeded its constitutional or statutory authority, made an erroneous interpretation of the law, acted in an arbitrary and capricious manner, or made a determination which is unsupported by the evidence in the record, the court may reverse the department's determination.

Filing the petition for appeal shall not stay the revocation.

Any person whose license has been suspended is entitled to judicial review under (cite law comparable to §15 of the Model State Administrative Procedure Act).

CHAPTER 6—ARTICLE III—VIOLATION OF LICENSE PROVISIONS

SECTION 6-303. Driving while license suspended or revoked.

(a) Any person who drives a motor vehicle on any highway of this State at a time when such person's privilege to do so is suspended or revoked shall be guilty of a misdemeanor and upon conviction shall be punished by imprisonment for not less than two days nor more than six months and there may be imposed in addition thereto a fine of not more than $500.

(b) Upon receiving a record of conviction of any driver for violating subsection (a) or any law or ordinance regulating the operation of motor vehicles where the offense was committed at a time when such person's license was suspended or revoked, the department may extend the period of suspension or revocation for an additional period of one year from and after the date upon which the period of suspension or revocation would otherwise have terminated.

CHAPTER 6—ARTICLE V—COMMERCIAL DRIVER'S LICENSE ACT

SECTION 6-514. Disqualification and cancellation.

(a) Disqualification Offenses. Any person is disqualified from driving a commercial motor vehicle for a period of not less than one year if convicted of a first violation of:

1. Driving or being in the actual physical control of a commercial motor vehicle under the influence of alcohol; or

2. Driving or being in the actual physical control of a commercial motor vehicle under the influence of any other drug or combination of other drugs to a degree which render the person incapable of safely driving; or

3. Driving or being in the actual physical control of a commercial motor vehicle under the combined influence of alcohol and any other drug or drugs to a degree which renders the person incapable of safely driving; or

4. Driving or being in the actual physical control of a commercial motor vehicle while the alcohol concentration of the person's blood or breath is 0.04 or more as defined by this code: or

5. Leaving the scene of an accident when that person is driving a commercial motor vehicle; or

6. Using a commercial motor vehicle in the commission of any felony; or

7. Refusal to submit to a test or tests to determine the driver's alcohol concentration or presence of other drugs while driving a commercial motor vehicle. If any of the above violations occur while transporting a hazardous material required to be placarded, the person shall be disqualified for a period of not less than three years.

(b) A person is disqualified for life for a second conviction of any of the offenses specified in paragraph (a), or any combination of those offenses, arising from 2 or more separate incidents.

(c) The department may issue regulations establishing guidelines, including conditions, under which a disqualification for life under paragraph (b) may be reduced to a period of not less than ten years.

(d) A person is disqualified from driving a commercial motor vehicle for life who uses a commercial motor vehicle in the commission of any felony involving the manufacture, distribution, or dispensing of a controlled substance, or possession with intent to manufacture, distribute or dispense a controlled substance.

(e) A person is disqualified from driving a commercial motor vehicle for a period of not less than 60 days if convicted of 2 serious traffic violations, committed in a commercial motor vehicle, arising from separate incidents, occurring within a 3-year period. However, a person will be disqualified from driving a commercial motor vehicle for a period of not less than 120 days if convicted of 3 serious traffic violations, committed in a commercial motor vehicle arising from separate incidents, occurring within a 3-year period.

(f) After suspending, revoking, or canceling a commercial driver license, the department shall update the driver's records to reflect that action within 10 days. After suspending or revoking the driving privilege of any person who has been issued a CDL or commercial driver instruction permit from another jurisdiction, the department shall notify the licensing authority of the state which issued the CDL or commercial driver instruction permit within 10 days.

SECTION 6-516. Prohibited alcohol offenses for commercial motor vehicle drivers.

(a) Notwithstanding any other provisions of this code, a person shall not drive a commercial motor vehicle within this state while having any measurable or detectable amount of alcohol in such person's system.

(b) A person who drives a commercial motor vehicle within this state while having any measurable or detectable amount of alcohol in such person's system, or who refuses to submit to an alcohol test under §6-517 of this Chapter, must be placed out of service for 24 hours.

(c) Any person who drives a commercial motor vehicle within this state with an alcohol concentration of 0.04 or more shall, in addition to any other sanctions which may be imposed under this code, be disqualified from driving a commercial motor vehicle under §6-514 of this Chapter.

SECTION 6-517. Implied consent requirements for commercial motor vehicle drivers.

(a) A person who drives a commercial motor vehicle within this state is deemed to have given consent, subject to administrative procedures established in this code, to take a test or tests of that person's blood, breath or urine for the purpose of determining that person's alcohol concentration or the presence of other drugs.

(b) A test or tests may be administered at the direction of a law enforcement officer, who after stopping or detaining the commercial motor vehicle driver, has probable cause to believe that driver was driving a commercial motor vehicle while having alcohol or drugs in such driver's system.

(c) A person requested to submit to a test or tests as provided in Subsection (a) above must be warned by the law enforcement officer requesting the test or tests, that a refusal to submit to the test or tests will result in that person being immediately placed out-of-service for a period of 24 hours and may result in being disqualified from operating a commercial motor vehicle for a period of not less than 12 months.

(d) If the person refuses testing, or submits to a test which discloses alcohol concentration of 0.04 or more, the law enforcement officer must submit a sworn report to the department certifying that the test was requested pursuant to Subsection (a) and that the person refused to submit to testing, or submitted to a test which disclosed an alcohol concentration of 0.04 or more.

(e) Upon receipt of the sworn report of a law enforcement officer submitted under Subsection (d), the department must disqualify the driver from driving a commercial motor vehicle under §6-514 of this Chapter.

SECTION 6-518. Notification of traffic convictions.

Within ten days after receiving a report of the conviction of any non-resident holder of a commercial driver license for any violation of state law or local ordinance relating to motor vehicle traffic control, other than parking violations, committed in a commercial motor vehicle, the department must notify the driver licensing authority in the licensing state of the conviction.

CHAPTER 10—ACCIDENTS AND ACCIDENT REPORTS

SECTION 10-102-Accidents involving death or personal injury

(a) The driver of any vehicle involved in an accident resulting in injury to or death of any person shall immediately stop such vehicle at the scene of such accident or as close thereto as possible but shall then forthwith return to and in every event shall remain at the scene of the accident until such driver has fulfilled the requirements of §10-104. Every such stop shall be made without obstructing traffic more than is necessary.

(b) Any person failing to stop or to comply with said requirements under such circumstances shall, upon conviction, be punished by imprisonment for not less than 30 days nor more than one year or by fine of not less than $100 nor more than $5,000 or by both such fine and imprisonment.

SECTION 10-104. Duty to give information and render aid.

(a) The driver of any vehicle involved in an accident resulting in injury to or death of any person or damage to any vehicle or other property which is driven or attended by any person shall give the driver's name, address and the registration number and owner of the vehicle the driver is operating and shall upon request and if available exhibit such driver's license or permit to drive to any person injured in such accident or to the driver or occupant of or person attending any vehicle or other property damaged in such accident and shall give such information and upon request exhibit such license or permit to any police officer at the scene of the accident or who is investigating the accident and shall render to any person injured in such accident reasonable assistance, including the carrying, or the making of arrangements for the carrying, of such person to a physician, surgeon, or hospital for medical or surgical treatment if it is apparent that such treatment is necessary, or if such carrying is requested by the injured person.

(b) In the event that none of the persons specified are in condition to receive the information to which they otherwise would be entitled under subdivision (a) of this section, and no police officer is present, the driver of any vehicle involved in such accident after fulfilling all other requirements of §10-102 and subdivision (a) of this section, insofar as possible on his or her part to be performed, shall forthwith report such accident to the nearest office of a duly authorized police authority and submit thereto the information specified in subdivision (a) of this section.

SECTION 10-116. Chemical tests in fatal crashes.

(a) When an accident results in the death of any driver or pedestrian within four hours of the accident, the medical examiner (or official performing like functions) shall withdraw blood or another bodily substance from the deceased driver or pedestrian so the amount of alcohol or the presence of other drugs in such person's blood can be determined. When possible, the withdrawal shall occur within eight hours of death.

(b) Subsection (a) shall not require withdrawing blood or any other bodily substance from a pedestrian who was less than 16 years of age at the time of such person's death.

(c) The medical examiner (or official performing like functions) or an approved laboratory shall analyze the blood or other substance to determine the amount of alcohol or the presence of other drugs in the dead driver's or pedestrian's blood.

(d) The results of the analysis required by this section shall be reported to the department and may be used by state and local officials only for statistical purposes that do not reveal the identity of the deceased person. Nothing in this subsection shall restrict the tests as evidence in criminal or civil proceedings.

(e) Withdrawal of blood or another bodily substance and its analysis shall comply with requirements of the (State Department of Health).

CHAPTER 11—ARTICLE IX—SERIOUS TRAFFIC OFFENSES

SECTION 11-902. Driving while under the influence of alcohol or drugs.

(a) A person shall not drive or be in actual physical control of any vehicle while:

1. The alcohol concentration in such person's blood or breath is 0.08 or more based on the definition of blood and breath units in §11-903(a) (5);

OPTIONAL I. The alcohol concentration in such person's blood or breath as measured within three hours of the time of driving or being in the actual physical control is 0.08 or more based on the definition of blood and breath units in §11-903. If proven by a preponderance of evidence, it shall be an affirmative defense to a violation of this subsection that the defendant consumed a sufficient quantity of alcohol after the time of driving or actual physical control of a vehicle and before the administration of the evidentiary test to cause the defendant's alcohol concentration to be 0.08 or more. The foregoing provision shall not limit the introduction of any other competent evidence bearing upon the question whether or not the person violated this section, including tests obtained more than three hours after such alleged violation.

2. Under the influence of alcohol;

3. Under the influence of any other drug or combination of other drugs to a degree which renders such person incapable of safely driving; or

4. Under the combined influence of alcohol and any other drug or drugs to a degree which renders such person incapable of safely driving.

(b) The fact that any person charged with violating this section is or has been legally entitled to use alcohol or other drug shall not constitute a defense against any charge of violating this section.

(c) In addition to the provisions of §11-904, every person convicted of violating this section shall be punished by imprisonment for not less than 10 days or more than one year, or by fine of not less than $100 nor more than $1,000, or by both such fine and imprisonment and on a second or subsequent conviction, such person shall be punished by imprisonment for not less than 90 days nor more than one year, and, in the discretion of the court, a fine of not more than $1,000.

SECTION 11-903. Chemical and other test.

(a) Upon the trial of any civil or criminal action or proceeding arising out of acts alleged to have been committed by any person while driving or in actual physical control of a vehicle while under the influence of alcohol or other drugs, evidence of the concentration of alcohol or other drugs in a person's blood or breath at the time alleged, as determined by analysis of the person's blood, urine, breath or other bodily substance, shall be admissible, Where such a test is made the following provisions shall apply:

1. Chemical analyses of the person's blood, urine, breath, or other bodily substance to be considered valid under the provisions of this section shall have been performed according to methods approved by the (State Department of Health) and by an individual possessing a valid permit issued by the (State Department of Health) for this purpose. The (State Department of Health) is authorized to approve satisfactory techniques or methods, to ascertain the qualifications and competence of individuals to conduct such analyses, and to issue permits which shall be subject to termination or revocation at the discretion of the (State Department of Health).

2. When a person shall submit to a blood test at the request of a law enforcement officer under the provisions of §6-207 or 6-210, only a physician or a registered nurse (or other qualified person) may withdraw blood for the purpose of determining the alcoholic or other drug content therein. This limitation shall not apply to the taking of breath or urine specimens.

3. The person tested may have a physician, or a qualified technician, chemist, registered nurse, or other qualified person of such person's own choosing administer a chemical test or tests in addition to any administered at the direction of a law enforcement officer. The failure or inability to obtain an additional test by a person shall not preclude the admission of evidence relating to the test or tests taken at the direction of a law enforcement officer.

4. Upon the request of the person who shall submit to a chemical test or tests at the request of a law enforcement officer, full information

concerning the test or tests shall be made available to the person or such person's attorney.

5. Alcohol concentration shall mean either grams of alcohol per 100 milliliters of blood or grams of alcohol per 210 liters of breath.

(b) Upon the trial of any civil or criminal action or proceeding arising out of acts alleged to have been committed by any person while driving or in actual physical control of a vehicle while under the influence of alcohol, the concentration of alcohol in the person's blood or breath at the time alleged as shown by analysis of the person's blood, urine, breath, or other bodily substance shall give rise to the following presumptions:

1. If there was at that time an alcohol concentration less than 0.08, such fact shall not give rise to any presumption that the person was or was not under the influence of alcohol, but such fact may be considered with other competent evidence in determining whether the person was under the influence of alcohol.

2. If there was at that time an alcohol concentration of 0.08 or more, it shall be presumed that the person was under the influence of alcohol.

3. The foregoing provisions of this subsection shall not be construed as limiting the introduction of any other competent evidence bearing upon the question whether the person was under the influence of alcohol.

(c) If a person under arrest refuses to submit to a chemical test under the provisions of §6-207, evidence of refusal shall be admissible in any civil or criminal action or proceeding arising out of acts alleged to have been committed while the person was driving or in actual physical control of a motor vehicle while under the influence of alcohol or other drugs.

SECTION 11-904. Post conviction examination and remedies.

(a) Before sentencing any person convicted of violating §11-902, the court shall conduct or order an appropriate examination or examinations to determine whether the person needs or would benefit from treatment for alcohol or other drug abuse.

(b) In addition to the penalties imposed by §11-902(c), and after receiving the results of the examination in subsection (a) or, upon a hearing and determination that the person is an habitual user of alcohol or other drugs, the court may order supervised treatment on an outpatient basis, or upon additional determinations that the person constitutes a danger to self or others and that adequate treatment facilities are available, the court may order such person committed for treatment at a facility or institution approved by the (State Department of Health).

(c) Any person subject to this section may be examined by a physician of such person's own choosing and the results of any such examination shall be considered by the court.

(d) No commitment or supervised treatment on an outpatient basis ordered under subsection (b) shall exceed one year. Upon motion duly made by the convicted person, an attorney, a relative or an attending physician, the court at any time after an order of commitment shall review said order. After determining the progress of treatment, the court may order its continuation or the court may order the person's release, supervised treatment on an outpatient basis, or it may impose penalties specified by this code giving credit for the time of commitment.

(e) Upon application by any person under an order of commitment or supervised treatment for a driver's license, the results of the examination referred to in subsection (a) and a report of the progress of the treatment ordered shall be forwarded by the applicant to the department for consideration by the health advisory board (appointed under §6-119).

(f) The department may after receiving the advice of the health advisory board issue a license to such person with conditions and restrictions consistent with the person's rehabilitation and with protection of the public notwithstanding the provisions of §6-214.

SECTION 11-905. Limits on Plea Bargaining.

When the prosecution agrees to a plea of guilty or nolo contendere to a charge of a violation other than §11-902(a) in satisfaction of, or as a substitute for, an original charge of a violation of §11-902(a), the prosecution shall state for the record a factual basis for the satisfaction, or substitution, including whether or not there had been consumption of any alcoholic beverage or ingestion or administration of any other drug, or both, by the defendant in connection with the offense.

SECTION 11-906. Homicide by vehicle.

(a) Whoever shall unlawfully and unintentionally cause the death of another person while engaged in the violation of any state law or municipal ordinance applying to the operation or use of a vehicle or to the regulation of traffic shall be guilty of homicide when such violation is the proximate cause of said death.

(b) Any person convicted of homicide by vehicle shall be fined not less than $500 nor more than $2,000, or shall be imprisoned in the county jail not less than three months nor more than one year, or may be so fined and so imprisoned, or shall be imprisoned in the penitentiary for a term not less than one year nor more than five years.

ARTICLE XII—OPERATION OF BICYCLES, OTHER HUMAN-POWERED VEHICLES, AND MOPEDS

SECTION 11-1202. Traffic laws apply to persons on bicycles and other human powered vehicles.

Every person propelling a vehicle by human power or riding a bicycle shall have all of the rights and all of the duties applicable to the driver of any other vehicle under Chapters 10 and 11, except as to special regulation sin this article and except as to those provisions which by their nature can have no application.

ARTICLE XIII—SPECIAL RULES FOR MOTORCYCLES

SECTION 11-1301. Traffic laws apply to persons operating motorcycles.

Every person operating a motorcycle shall be granted all of the rights and shall be subject to all of the duties applicable to the driver of any other vehicle under this code, except as to special regulations in this article and except as to those provisions of this code which by their nature can have no application.

ARTICLE XV—VICTIMS OF A TRAFFIC-RELATED OFFENSE

Section 11-1502. Rights of victims.

Victims shall have the following rights:

(a) To speedy prosecution of the offense. In any criminal justice proceeding, the police, the prosecutor, and the court shall take appropriate action to ensure speedy prosecution of the defendant. Victims shall be informed by the prosecuting attorney of any motions which would result in delay of the prosecution and be allowed to object in writing.

(b) Upon request by the victim, to be informed by the police investigating the case of the status of the investigation, and by the prosecuting attorney prior to any critical decisions concerning the case including the charging decision, diversion, dismissal, or other disposition.

(c) To be present at any time the defendant has the right to be present during all criminal justice proceedings related to an offense unless the court determines that exclusion is necessary to protect the confidentiality of juvenile or similar proceedings. If a victim is unable to attend the court proceedings, the court may designate a representative of the victim who has the same right to be present as the victim would have had.

(d) To make victim impact statements to the court including information about the financial, emotional, psychological, and physical effects of the crime on the victim, the circumstances surrounding the crime, the manner in which it was perpetrated, and the victim's opinion of any recommended sentence of the convicted offender. A victim may present an impact statement to the court either orally or in writing.

(e) To an order of restitution if the order is authorized by the laws of this state.

SECTION 11-1503. Law Enforcement Agency.

(a) At the time of the initial contact between any law enforcement agency and the victim, the law enforcement agency investigating the case shall provide the victim a written statement of rights which shall include the following information:

1. A statement and explanation of the victim's rights as enumerated by §11-1502 of this code;

2. The availability of victim assistance, medical and emergency services;

3. The availability of victim compensation benefits, including the name, office address, and telephone number of the contact person(s) responsible for administering the program; and

4. The office addresses and telephone numbers of appropriate victim support and services groups.

(b) As soon as available, the police shall provide to the victim the following:

1. The office address and telephone number of the prosecutor's office;

2. The case number and the names, office addresses, and telephone numbers of the law enforcement officers assigned to investigate the case; and

3. If known, whether the suspect has been taken into custody, and if taken into custody, whether released, and any conditions attached to the release.

SECTION 11-1504. Prosecutor.

(a) Upon request by the victim for information concerning the criminal court proceedings, a prosecuting attorney shall inform the victim of the following:

1. A statement and explanation of the victim's rights as enumerated by §11-1502;

2. The actual assignment of the case, including case number, and the court to which it is assigned;

3. The date, time, and location of any criminal proceedings relative to the offense;

4. The availability of crime victim compensation benefits, including the name, office address, and telephone numbers of contact persons responsible for administering the program;

5. The availability of any transportation services to court proceedings;

6. Whether the defendant has a right to review the pre-sentence reports and impact statements;

7. Whether the defendant has the right to attend and make a statement at the sentencing hearing;

8. The time and place of any hearing for the reconsideration of the sentence imposed; and

9. The right to receive information from corrections officials concerning imprisonment and release.

10. If the defendant appeals, the prosecutor shall inform the victim of the status of the case on appeal and the decision of the appellate court upon disposition.

(b) The prosecutor shall notify the victim in writing of the date, time, and location of the sentencing hearing and advise the victim of the opportunity to present a victim's impact statement or to appear at the sentencing proceeding.

SECTION 11-1505. Probation Department.

The Probation Department, in preparing any pre-sentence report on the defendant, must attempt to consult with the victim and must include a written victim impact statement as part of the pre-sentence report if the victim chooses to submit one. If the victim cannot be located or declines to cooperate, the probation officer must include a notation to that effect in the report.

SECTION 11-1506. Court.

The Court shall orally inform victims present at the sentencing hearing of their right to present victim impact statements.

CHAPTER 16—ARTICLE I—PARTIES TO CRIME, OWNERS, AND PUBLIC EMPLOYEES

SECTION 16-101. Parties to a crime.

Every person who commits, attempts to commit, conspires to commit, or aids or abets in the commission of, any act declared in this code to be a crime, whether individually or in connection with one or more other persons or as a principal, agent or accessory, shall be guilty of such offense, and every person who falsely, fraudulently, forcibly or willfully induces, causes, coerces, requires, permits or directs another to violate any provision of this code is likewise guilty of such offense.

16-102. Offenses by persons owning or controlling vehicles.

It is unlawful for the owner, or any other person, employing or otherwise directing the driver of any vehicle to require or knowingly to permit the operation of such vehicle upon a highway in any manner contrary to law.

SECTION 16-103. Public officers and employees-exceptions

The provisions of chapters 10, 11, 12, 13 and 14 applicable to drivers of vehicles upon the highways shall apply to the drivers of all vehicles owned or operated by the United States, this State or any county, city, town, district or any other political subdivision of the State, subject to such specific exceptions as are set forth in this code.

ARTICLE II—ARRESTS AND ISSUANCE OF CITATIONS

SECTION 16-201. Procedure upon arrest for felony.

Whenever a person is arrested for any violation of this code declared herein to be a felony, such person shall be dealt with in like manner as upon arrest for the commission of any other felony. For the purposes of this section any offense which may be punishable by imprisonment in a state penitentiary is a felony.

Section 16-202. Arrests for serious offenses.

(a) The authority of a police officer to make an arrest is the same as upon an arrest for a felony when such officer has reasonable and probable grounds to believe that the person arrested has committed any of the following offenses:

1. Homicide by vehicle;

2. Driving or being in actual physical control of a vehicle while under the influence of alcohol or any drug as prohibited by §11-902.

3. Failure to stop, or failure to give information, or failure to render reasonable assistance, in the event of an accident resulting in death or personal injuries, as prescribed in §10-102 and 10-104.

4. Failure to stop, or failure to give information, in the event of an accident resulting in damage to a vehicle or to other property, as prescribed in §10-103 to 10-105 inclusive;

5. Reckless driving;

6. Racing on the highway; or

7. Willfully fleeing from or attempting to elude a police officer. Provided, however, that the manner of making arrests under this section shall be as in misdemeanor cases.

(b) Whenever any person is arrested as authorized in this section such person shall be taken without unnecessary delay before the proper magistrate as specified in §10-208, except that in the case of the offenses designated in paragraphs 4, 5, 6 and 7, a police officer shall have the same discretion as is provided in other cases in §16-204.

CHAPTER 17—ARTICLE II—FELONIES

SECTION 17-201. Penalty for felony.

Any person who is convicted of a violation of any of the provisions of this code herein or by the laws of this State declared to constitute a felony shall be punished by imprisonment for not less than one year nor more than five years, or by a fine of not less than $500 nor more than $5,000, or by both such fine and imprisonment.

CHAPTER 17—ARTICLE III—REGISTRATION

SECTION 17-301. Suspension of registration.

Upon conviction of any of the following offenses the court may, in addition to other penalties prescribed by this code, suspend the registration of any vehicle or vehicles registered in the name of the person convicted for a period of not to exceed [period of time] and any such suspension shall be immediately reported by the court to the department:

1. Homicide by vehicle (manslaughter resulting from the operation of a motor vehicle);

2. Driving or being in actual physical control of a motor vehicle while under the influence of alcohol or any drug;

3. Any felony in the commission of which a motor vehicle is used;

4. Failure to stop, render aid or identify oneself as required by §10-102 in the event of a motor vehicle accident resulting in death or personal injury;

5. Unauthorized use of a motor vehicle belonging to another;

6. Driving while the privilege to do so is suspended or revoked;

7. Racing on a highway;

8. Willfully fleeing from or attempting to elude a police officer; or

9. Any offense punishable under §17-201.

Source: National Committee on Uniform Traffic Laws and Ordinances (NCUTLO).

APPENDIX 16:
PERCENT OF FATALLY INJURED PEOPLE WITH A BAC LEVEL OF 0.08% OR GREATER (1992-2002)

YEAR	ALL DRIVERS	PASSENGER VEHICLE DRIVERS	TRACTOR-TRAILER DRIVERS	MOTORCYCLISTS	PEDESTRIANS
1992	37	38	5	42	39
1993	36	37	4	39	39
1994	33	34	6	33	37
1995	34	35	5	34	37
1996	33	34	5	36	39
1997	32	33	3	33	35
1998	32	32	4	35	37
1999	31	32	3	33	38
2000	32	33	3	33	37
2001	32	33	3	30	36
2002	32	33	6	32	36

Source: Insurance Institute for Highway Safety.

APPENDIX 17:
PERCENT OF FATALLY INJURED PEOPLE WITH A BAC LEVEL OF 0.15% OR GREATER (1992-2002)

YEAR	ALL DRIVERS	PASSENGER VEHICLE DRIVERS	TRACTOR-TRAILER DRIVERS	MOTORCYCLISTS	PEDESTRIANS
1992	28	28	3	28	31
1993	26	27	2	24	32
1994	25	26	4	21	29
1995	25	26	3	21	29
1996	24	25	4	23	31
1997	23	24	2	21	29
1998	23	24	3	22	29
1999	22	23	2	20	30
2000	23	24	1	21	29
2001	23	24	2	18	28
2002	23	24	3	18	29

Source: Insurance Institute for Highway Safety.

APPENDIX 18:
ILLEGAL BLOOD ALCOHOL CONCENTRATION (BAC) LEVELS BY STATE

STATE	BAC DEFINED AS ILLEGAL PER SE*
Alabama	0.08
Alaska	0.08
Arizona	0.08
Arkansas	0.08
California	0.08
Colorado	0.08
Connecticut	0.08
Delaware	0.08
District of Columbia	0.08
Florida	0.08
Georgia	0.08
Hawaii	0.08
Idaho	0.08
Illinois	0.08
Indiana	0.08
Iowa	0.08
Kansas	0.08
Kentucky	0.08
Louisiana	0.08
Maine	0.08
Maryland	0.08
Massachusetts	0.08
Michigan	0.08
Minnesota	0.10**
Mississippi	0.08

STATE	BAC DEFINED AS ILLEGAL PER SE*
Missouri	0.08
Montana	0.08
Nebraska	0.08
Nevada	0.08
New Hampshire	0.08
New Jersey	0.08
New Mexico	0.08
New York	0.08
North Carolina	0.08
North Dakota	0.08
Ohio	0.08
Oklahoma	0.08
Oregon	0.08
Pennsylvania	0.08
Rhode Island	0.08
South Carolina	0.08
South Dakota	0.08
Tennessee	0.08
Texas	0.08
Utah	0.08
Vermont	0.08
Virginia	0.08
Washington	0.08
West Virginia	0.08
Wisconsin	0.08
Wyoming	0.08

* Information pertains to drivers in violation of the BAC defined as illegal per se for all drivers, not the special BAC for young drivers.

** Minnesota has passed legislation to lower their BAC limit to 0.08% effective August 1, 2005.

Source: Insurance Institute for Highway Safety.

APPENDIX 19:
STATES WITH MANDATORY BLOOD
ALCOHOL CONCENTRATION (BAC)
LEVEL TESTING

STATE	MANDATORY TESTING
ALABAMA	NO
ALASKA	YES
ARIZONA	NO
ARKANSAS	YES
CALIFORNIA	YES
COLORADO	YES
CONNECTICUT	YES
DELAWARE	YES
DISTRICT OF COLUMBIA	YES
FLORIDA	YES
GEORGIA	NO
HAWAII	YES
IDAHO	YES
ILLINOIS	YES
INDIANA	YES
IOWA	YES
KANSAS	YES
KENTUCKY	YES
LOUISIANA	YES
MAINE	YES
MARYLAND	YES
MASSACHUSETTS	NO

STATE	MANDATORY TESTING
MICHIGAN	YES
MINNESOTA	YES
MISSISSIPPI	YES
MISSOURI	YES
MONTANA	NO
NEBRASKA	YES
NEVADA	YES
NEW HAMPSHIRE	NO
NEW JERSEY	YES
NEW MEXICO	YES
NEW YORK	YES
NORTH CAROLINA	YES
NORTH DAKOTA	YES
OHIO	NO
OKLAHOMA	YES
OREGON	NO
PENNSYLVANIA	NO
RHODE ISLAND	NO
SOUTH CAROLINA	NO
SOUTH DAKOTA	YES
TENNESSEE	NO
TEXAS	YES
UTAH	YES
VERMONT	NO
VIRGINIA	NO
WASHINGTON	YES
WEST VIRGINIA	NO
WISCONSIN	YES
WYOMING	YES

Source: Mothers Against Drunk Driving (MADD).

APPENDIX 20:
STATES WITH SOBRIETY CHECKPOINTS

STATE	SOBRIETY CHECKPOINTS
ALABAMA	YES
ALASKA	NO
ARIZONA	YES
ARKANSAS	YES
CALIFORNIA	YES
COLORADO	YES
CONNECTICUT	YES
DELAWARE	YES
DISTRICT OF COLUMBIA	YES
FLORIDA	YES
GEORGIA	YES
HAWAII	YES
IDAHO	NO
ILLINOIS	YES
INDIANA	YES
IOWA	YES
KANSAS	YES
KENTUCKY	YES
LOUISIANA	NO
MAINE	YES
MARYLAND	YES
MASSACHUSETTS	YES
MICHIGAN	NO
MINNESOTA	NO
MISSISSIPPI	YES

STATE	SOBRIETY CHECKPOINTS
MISSOURI	YES
MONTANA	YES
NEBRASKA	YES
NEVADA	NO
NEW HAMPSHIRE	YES
NEW JERSEY	YES
NEW MEXICO	YES
NEW YORK	YES
NORTH CAROLINA	NO
NORTH DAKOTA	YES
OHIO	YES
OKLAHOMA	YES
OREGON	NO
PENNSYLVANIA	YES
RHODE ISLAND	NO
SOUTH CAROLINA	YES
SOUTH DAKOTA	YES
TENNESSEE	YES
TEXAS	NO
UTAH	YES
VERMONT	YES
VIRGINIA	YES
WASHINGTON	NO
WEST VIRGINIA	YES
WISCONSIN	NO
WYOMING	NO

Source: Mothers Against Drunk Driving (MADD).

APPENDIX 21:
PERCENT OF FATALLY INJURED PASSENGER VEHICLE DRIVERS AGE 16-20 WITH A BAC LEVEL OF 0.08% OR GREATER (1992-2002)

YEAR	AGE 16-17	AGE 18-20
1992	18	37
1993	16	34
1994	17	32
1995	15	29
1996	17	30
1997	17	31
1998	15	30
1999	16	31
2000	16	30
2001	13	31
2002	14	30

Source: Insurance Institute for Highway Safety.

APPENDIX 22:
CUMULATIVE ESTIMATED NUMBER OF LIVES SAVED BY MINIMUM AGE DRINKING LAWS (1975-2002)

YEAR	NUMBER OF LIVES SAVED
1975-1994	14,816
1995	15,667
1996	16,513
1997	17,359
1998	18,220
1999	19,121
2000	20,043
2001	20,970
2002	21,887

Source: National Highway Transportation Safety Administration.

APPENDIX 23:
ALCOHOL INVOLVEMENT AMONG DRIVERS AGE 16 TO 20, BY AGE AND DRIVER'S BAC (2001)

AGE	TOTAL	NO ALCOHOL (0.00)	0.01-0.07	0.08 AND GREATER
16	1009	879 (87%)	45 (4%)	85 (8%)
17	1437	1190 (83%)	71 (5%)	177 (12%)
18	1840	1437 (78%)	98 (5%)	305 (17%)
19	1926	1417 (74%)	110 (6%)	399 (21%)
20	1751	1202 (69%)	97 (6%)	453 (26%)

Source: National Highway Transportation Safety Administration.

APPENDIX 24:
STATE ILLEGAL PER SE
BLOOD ALCOHOL CONCENTRATION (BAC)
LEVELS—YOUNG DRIVERS (UNDER 21)

STATE	ILLEGAL PER SE BAC LEVEL
ALABAMA	0.02
ALASKA	0.00
ARIZONA	0.00
ARKANSAS	0.02
CALIFORNIA	0.01
COLORADO	0.02
CONNECTICUT	0.02
DELAWARE	0.02
DISTRICT OF COLUMBIA	0.02
FLORIDA	0.02
GEORGIA	0.02
HAWAII	0.02
IDAHO	0.02
ILLINOIS	0.00
INDIANA	0.02
IOWA	0.02
KANSAS	0.02
KENTUCKY	0.02
LOUISIANA	0.02
MAINE	0.00
MARYLAND	0.02
MASSACHUSETTS	0.02

STATE	ILLEGAL PER SE BAC LEVEL
MICHIGAN	0.02
MINNESOTA	0.00
MISSISSIPPI	0.08
MISSOURI	0.02
MONTANA	0.02
NEBRASKA	0.02
NEVADA	0.02
NEW HAMPSHIRE	0.02
NEW JERSEY	0.01
NEW MEXICO	0.02
NEW YORK	0.02
NORTH CAROLINA	0.00
NORTH DAKOTA	0.02
OHIO	0.02
OKLAHOMA	0.00
OREGON	0.00
PENNSYLVANIA	0.02
RHODE ISLAND	0.02
SOUTH CAROLINA	0.02
SOUTH DAKOTA	0.02
TENNESSEE	0.02
TEXAS	0.00
UTAH	0.00
VERMONT	0.02
VIRGINIA	0.02
WASHINGTON	0.02
WEST VIRGINIA	0.02
WISCONSIN	0.02
WYOMING	0.02

Source: Insurance Institute for Highway Safety.

APPENDIX 25:
STATE YOUNG DRIVERS LAWS

STATE	MINIMUM AGE-LEARNER'S PERMIT (LP)	MINIMUM AGE-REGULAR LICENSE	LP REQUIRED BEFORE REGULAR LICENSE	MINIMUM LP PERIOD	LP EXPIRATION	NIGHT DRIVING RESTRICTIONS	SEE FOOTNOTE
ALABAMA	15	16	NO	N/A	4 YEARS	NO	N/A
ALASKA	14	16	NO	N/A	2 YEARS	NO	N/A
ARIZONA	15-6MOS	16	NO	N/A	1 YEAR	NO	N/A
ARKANSAS	14	16	YES	30 DAYS	60 DAYS	NO	N/A
CALIFORNIA	15-6MOS	16	YES	180 DAYS	1 YEAR	MIDNIGHT -5AM UNTIL AGE 17	N/A
COLORADO	15-3MOS	16	YES	90 DAYS	8 MONTHS	NO	N/A

STATE	MINIMUM AGE-LEARNER'S PERMIT (LP)	MINIMUM AGE-REGULAR LICENSE	LP REQUIRED BEFORE REGULAR LICENSE	MINIMUM LP PERIOD	LP EXPIRATION	NIGHT DRIVING RESTRICTIONS	SEE FOOTNOTE
CONNECTICUT	16	16-6MOS	YES	180 DAYS	UNTIL AGE 18	NO	1
DELAWARE	15-10MOS	16	NO	N/A	760 DAYS	NO	N/A
DISTRICT OF COLUMBIA	16	16	YES	N/A	3 MONTHS	NO	N/A
FLORIDA	15	16	YES	180 DAYS	6 YEARS	11PM-6AM AT AGE 16; 1-5 AM AT AGE 17	N/A
GEORGIA	15	16	YES	1 YEAR	2 YEARS	1-5AM UNTIL AGE 18	N/A
HAWAII	15	15	YES	90 DAYS	180 DAYS	NO	N/A
IDAHO	15	15	NO	N/A	180 DAYS	NO	N/A
ILLINOIS	15	16	YES	90 DAYS	2 YEARS	11PM-6AM FROM MON-THURS AND MIDNIGHT TO 6AM FROM FRIDAY TO SUNDAY UNTIL AGE 17	N/A

STATE	MINIMUM AGE- LEARNER'S PERMIT (LP)	MINIMUM AGE- REGULAR LICENSE	LP REQUIRED BEFORE REGULAR LICENSE	MINIMUM LP PERIOD	LP EXPIRATION	NIGHT DRIVING RESTRICTIONS	SEE FOOTNOTE
INDIANA	15	16-1MO	YES	60 DAYS	UNTIL AGE 16-3MOS	NO	N/A
IOWA	14	16	YES	N/A	2 YEARS FROM BIRTHDAY IN YEAR OF ISSUANCE	NO	N/A
KANSAS	14	16	NO	N/A	1 YEAR	NO	N/A
KENTUCKY	16	16-6MOS	YES	180 DAYS	1 YEAR	NO	N/A
LOUISIANA	15	16	YES	90 DAYS	4 YEARS	11PM-5AM UNTIL AGE 17	N/A
MAINE	15	16	YES	90 DAYS	18 MONTHS	NO	N/A
MARYLAND	15-9MOS	16	YES	14 DAYS	180 DAYS	MIDNIGHT-5AM FOR 1 YEAR OR UNTIL AGE 18	N/A
MASSACHUSETTS	16	16-6MOS	YES	N/A	1 YEAR	1-4AM UNTIL AGE 18	N/A
MICHIGAN	15	16	YES	180 DAYS	1 YEAR	MIDNIGHT-5AM UNTIL AGE 17	N/A
MINNESOTA	15	16	YES	180 DAYS	1 YEAR	NO	N/A

STATE	MINIMUM AGE-LEARNER'S PERMIT (LP)	MINIMUM AGE-REGULAR LICENSE	LP REQUIRED BEFORE REGULAR LICENSE	MINIMUM LP PERIOD	LP EXPIRATION	NIGHT DRIVING RESTRICTIONS	SEE FOOTNOTE
MISSISSIPPI	15	16	YES	30 DAYS	1 YEAR	NO	N/A
MISSOURI	15-6MOS	16	NO	N/A	6 MONTHS	NO	N/A
MONTANA	14-6MOS	15	NO	N/A	6 MONTHS	NO	N/A
NEBRASKA	15	16	NO	N/A	1 YEAR	NO	N/A
NEVADA	15-6MOS	16	NO	N/A	8 MONTHS	NO	N/A
NEW HAMPSHIRE	16	16-3MOS	YES	90 DAYS	N/A	1-5AM UNTIL AGE 18	N/A
NEW JERSEY	16	17	YES	N/A	1 YEAR-3MOS	NO	N/A
NEW MEXICO	15	15	YES	N/A	6 MONTHS	NO	N/A
NEW YORK	16	16	YES	N/A	3 YEARS	9PM-5AM UNTIL AGE 18	2
NORTH CAROLINA	15	16	YES	1 YEAR	18 MONTHS	9PM-5AM FOR 6 MONTHS OR UNTIL AGE 18	N/A
NORTH DAKOTA	14	16	YES	90 DAYS	1 YEAR	NO	N/A
OHIO	15-6MOS	16	YES	6 MONTHS	1 YEAR	1AM-5AM UNTIL AGE 17	N/A
OKLAHOMA	15-6MOS	16	NO	N/A	4 YEARS	NO	N/A
OREGON	15	16	NO	N/A	18 MONTHS	NO	N/A

STATE	MINIMUM AGE-LEARNER'S PERMIT (LP)	MINIMUM AGE-REGULAR LICENSE	LP REQUIRED BEFORE REGULAR LICENSE	MINIMUM LP PERIOD	LP EXPIRATION	NIGHT DRIVING RESTRICTIONS	SEE FOOTNOTE
PENNSYLVANIA	16	16	YES	N/A	120 DAYS	MIDNIGHT-5AM UNTIL AGE 18	N/A
RHODE ISLAND	16	16	YES	N/A	180 DAYS	NO	N/A
SOUTH CAROLINA	15	15	YES	15 DAYS	12 MONTHS	6PM-6AM EST AND 8PM-6AM EDT UNTIL AGE 16	N/A
SOUTH DAKOTA	14	16	NO	N/A	180 DAYS	NO	4
TENNESSEE	15	16	NO	90 DAYS	1 YEAR	NO	3
TEXAS	15	16	YES	N/A	1 YEAR	NO	N/A
UTAH	16	16	YES	N/A	6 MONTHS	NO	5
VERMONT	15	16	YES	N/A	2 YEARS	NO	N/A
VIRGINIA	15	16	YES	180 DAYS	INDEFINITE	NO	N/A
WASHINGTON	15	16	YES	N/A	1 YEAR	NO	N/A
WEST VIRGINIA	15	16	YES	N/A	UNTIL AGE 16-2MOS	NO	N/A
WISCONSIN	15-6MOS	16	YES	N/A	6 MONTHS	NO	N/A
WYOMING	15	16	NO	10 DAYS	1 YEAR	NO	N/A

NOTES:

1. In Connecticut, the 180-day minimum learner's period is reduced to 120 days for applicants who have completed approved driver education.

2. In New York, licensing laws prohibit people with DJ licenses (16 and 17 year-olds) from driving in New York City.

3. In Tennessee, the 3-month minimum learner's period is waived for applicants who have completed approved driver education.

4. South Dakota issues a restricted license which allows 14 and 15 year-olds to drive unsupervised between the h ours of 6am to 8pm; at other times they are allowed to drive only under the supervision of a parent or guardian. The restricted license becomes a regular license when the holder turns 16.

5. In Utah, instructional permits also are issued to people 15 years and 9 months old. Valid for 1 year, these permit driving only with a professional driving instructor. Instructors may give practice permits, valid for 90 days, that allow driving only with a parent or guardian.

Source: Insurance Institute for Highway Safety.

APPENDIX 26:
STATE ADMINISTRATIVE LICENSE SUSPENSION PROVISIONS

STATE	FIRST OFFENSE ADMINISTRATIVE LICENSE SUSPENSION
Alabama	90 days
Alaska	90 days
Arizona	90 days
Arkansas	120 days
California	4 months
Colorado	3 months
Connecticut	90 days
Delaware	3 months
District of Columbia	2-90 days
Florida	6 months
Georgia	1 year
Hawaii	3 months
Idaho	90 days
Illinois	3 months
Indiana	180 days
Iowa	180 days
Kansas	30 days
Kentucky	n/a
Louisiana	90 days
Maine	90 days
Maryland	45 days
Massachusetts	90 days
Michigan	n/a

STATE	FIRST OFFENSE ADMINISTRATIVE LICENSE SUSPENSION
Minnesota	90 days
Mississippi	90 days
Missouri	30 days
Montana	n/a
Nebraska	90 days
Nevada	90 days
New Hampshire	6 months
New Jersey	n/a
New Mexico	90 days
New York	until prosecution complete
North Carolina	30 days
North Dakota	91 days
Ohio	90 days
Oklahoma	180 days
Oregon	90 days
Pennsylvania	n/a
Rhode Island	n/a
South Carolina	n/a
South Dakota	n/a
Tennessee	n/a
Texas	90 days
Utah	90 days
Vermont	90 days
Virginia	7 days
Washington	90 days
West Virginia	6 months
Wisconsin	6 months
Wyoming	90 days

Source: Insurance Institute for Highway Safety.

APPENDIX 27:
STATE LAWS CONCERNING RESTORATION
OF DRIVING PRIVILEGES
DURING SUSPENSION

STATE	DRIVING PRIVILEGES RESTORED DURING SUSPENSION PERIOD
Alabama	no
Alaska	after 30 days
Arizona	after 30 days
Arkansas	yes
California	after 30 days
Colorado	yes
Connecticut	yes
Delaware	no
District of Columbia	yes
Florida	yes
Georgia	yes
Hawaii	after 30 days
Idaho	after 30 days
Illinois	after 30 days
Indiana	after 30 days
Iowa	after 90 days
Kansas	no
Kentucky	n/a
Louisiana	after 30 days
Maine	yes
Maryland	yes

STATE	DRIVING PRIVILEGES RESTORED DURING SUSPENSION PERIOD
Massachusetts	no
Michigan	n/a
Minnesota	after 15 days
Mississippi	no
Missouri	no
Montana	n/a
Nebraska	after 30 days
Nevada	after 45 days
New Hampshire	no
New Jersey	n/a
New Mexico	after 30 days
New York	yes
North Carolina	after 10 days
North Dakota	after 30 days
Ohio	after 15 days
Oklahoma	yes
Oregon	after 30 days
Pennsylvania	n/a
Rhode Island	n/a
South Carolina	n/a
South Dakota	n/a
Tennessee	n/a
Texas	yes
Utah	no
Vermont	no
Virginia	no
Washington	after 30 days
West Virginia	after 30 days
Wisconsin	yes
Wyoming	yes

Source: Insurance Institute for Highway Safety.

APPENDIX 28:
STATES WITH VEHICLE LICENSE PLATE CONFISCATION LAWS

STATE	LICENSE PLATE CONFISCATION
ALABAMA	NO
ALASKA	NO
ARIZONA	YES
ARKANSAS	NO
CALIFORNIA	NO
COLORADO	NO
CONNECTICUT	NO
DELAWARE	NO
DISTRICT OF COLUMBIA	NO
FLORIDA	NO
GEORGIA	NO
HAWAII	NO
IDAHO	NO
ILLINOIS	NO
INDIANA	YES
IOWA	YES
KANSAS	NO
KENTUCKY	NO
LOUISIANA	NO
MAINE	YES
MARYLAND	NO
MASSACHUSETTS	NO
MICHIGAN	NO

STATE	LICENSE PLATE CONFISCATION
MINNESOTA	YES
MISSISSIPPI	NO
MISSOURI	NO
MONTANA	NO
NEBRASKA	NO
NEVADA	NO
NEW HAMPSHIRE	YES
NEW JERSEY	NO
NEW MEXICO	NO
NEW YORK	YES
NORTH CAROLINA	NO
NORTH DAKOTA	YES
OHIO	YES
OKLAHOMA	NO
OREGON	YES
PENNSYLVANIA	NO
RHODE ISLAND	YES
SOUTH CAROLINA	NO
SOUTH DAKOTA	YES
TENNESSEE	NO
TEXAS	NO
UTAH	NO
VERMONT	NO
VIRGINIA	YES
WASHINGTON	NO
WEST VIRGINIA	NO
WISCONSIN	NO
WYOMING	YES

Source: Mothers Against Drunk Driving (MADD).

APPENDIX 29:
STATE IGNITION INTERLOCK PROVISIONS

STATE	IGNITION INTERLOCK PROVISION
Alabama	no
Alaska	yes
Arizona	yes
Arkansas	yes
California	yes
Colorado	yes
Connecticut	no
Delaware	yes
District of Columbia	no
Florida	yes
Georgia	yes
Hawaii	yes
Idaho	yes
Illinois	yes
Indiana	yes
Iowa	yes
Kansas	yes
Kentucky	yes
Louisiana	yes
Maine	yes
Maryland	yes
Massachusetts	no
Michigan	yes

STATE	IGNITION INTERLOCK PROVISION
Minnesota	no
Mississippi	yes
Missouri	yes
Montana	yes
Nebraska	yes
Nevada	yes
New Hampshire	yes
New Jersey	yes
New Mexico	yes
New York	yes
North Carolina	yes
North Dakota	yes
Ohio	yes
Oklahoma	yes
Oregon	yes
Pennsylvania	yes
Rhode Island	yes
South Carolina	yes
South Dakota	no
Tennessee	yes
Texas	yes
Utah	yes
Vermont	no
Virginia	yes
Washington	yes
West Virginia	yes
Wisconsin	yes
Wyoming	no

Source: Insurance Institute for Highway Safety.

APPENDIX 30:
VEHICLE FORFEITURE PROVISIONS

STATE	FORFEITURE PROVISION
Alabama	no
Alaska	yes
Arizona	yes
Arkansas	yes
California	yes
Colorado	no
Connecticut	no
Delaware	no
District of Columbia	no
Florida	yes
Georgia	yes
Hawaii	no
Idaho	no
Illinois	yes
Indiana	no
Iowa	no
Kansas	no
Kentucky	yes
Louisiana	yes
Maine	yes
Maryland	no
Massachusetts	no
Michigan	yes
Minnesota	yes
Mississippi	yes

STATE	FORFEITURE PROVISION
Missouri	yes
Montana	yes
Nebraska	no
Nevada	no
New Hampshire	no
New Jersey	no
New Mexico	no
New York	yes
North Carolina	yes
North Dakota	yes
Ohio	yes
Oklahoma	yes
Oregon	yes
Pennsylvania	yes
Rhode Island	yes
South Carolina	yes
South Dakota	no
Tennessee	yes
Texas	yes
Utah	no
Vermont	yes
Virginia	yes
Washington	yes
West Virginia	no
Wisconsin	yes
Wyoming	no

Source: Insurance Institute for Highway Safety.

APPENDIX 31:
STATES WITH MANDATORY
IMPRISONMENT FOR FIRST DWI
CONVICTION

STATE	MANDATORY IMPRISONMENT
ALABAMA	NO
ALASKA	YES
ARIZONA	NO
ARKANSAS	NO
CALIFORNIA	NO
COLORADO	YES
CONNECTICUT	YES
DELAWARE	NO
DISTRICT OF COLUMBIA	NO
FLORIDA	NO
GEORGIA	YES
HAWAII	YES
IDAHO	NO
ILLINOIS	NO
INDIANA	NO
IOWA	YES
KANSAS	YES
KENTUCKY	YES
LOUISIANA	YES
MAINE	YES
MARYLAND	NO
MASSACHUSETTS	NO

STATE	MANDATORY IMPRISONMENT
MICHIGAN	NO
MINNESOTA	NO
MISSISSIPPI	NO
MISSOURI	NO
MONTANA	YES
NEBRASKA	NO
NEVADA	NO
NEW HAMPSHIRE	NO
NEW JERSEY	NO
NEW MEXICO	NO
NEW YORK	NO
NORTH CAROLINA	NO
NORTH DAKOTA	NO
OHIO	NO
OKLAHOMA	NO
OREGON	YES
PENNSYLVANIA	YES
RHODE ISLAND	NO
SOUTH CAROLINA	YES
SOUTH DAKOTA	NO
TENNESSEE	YES
TEXAS	NO
UTAH	YES
VERMONT	NO
VIRGINIA	NO
WASHINGTON	YES
WEST VIRGINIA	YES
WISCONSIN	NO
WYOMING	NO

Source: Mothers Against Drunk Driving (MADD).

APPENDIX 32:
STATES WITH MANDATORY
IMPRISONMENT FOR REPEAT DWI
OFFENSES

STATE	MANDATORY IMPRISONMENT
ALABAMA	YES
ALASKA	YES
ARIZONA	YES
ARKANSAS	YES
CALIFORNIA	YES
COLORADO	YES
CONNECTICUT	YES
DELAWARE	YES
DISTRICT OF COLUMBIA	NO
FLORIDA	YES
GEORGIA	YES
HAWAII	YES
IDAHO	YES
ILLINOIS	YES
INDIANA	YES
IOWA	YES
KANSAS	YES
KENTUCKY	YES
LOUISIANA	YES
MAINE	YES
MARYLAND	YES
MASSACHUSETTS	YES

STATE	MANDATORY IMPRISONMENT
MICHIGAN	YES
MINNESOTA	YES
MISSISSIPPI	NO
MISSOURI	YES
MONTANA	YES
NEBRASKA	YES
NEVADA	YES
NEW HAMPSHIRE	YES
NEW JERSEY	YES
NEW MEXICO	YES
NEW YORK	NO
NORTH CAROLINA	YES
NORTH DAKOTA	YES
OHIO	YES
OKLAHOMA	YES
OREGON	YES
PENNSYLVANIA	YES
RHODE ISLAND	YES
SOUTH CAROLINA	YES
SOUTH DAKOTA	NO
TENNESSEE	YES
TEXAS	YES
UTAH	YES
VERMONT	YES
VIRGINIA	YES
WASHINGTON	YES
WEST VIRGINIA	YES
WISCONSIN	YES
WYOMING	YES

Source: Mothers Against Drunk Driving (MADD).

APPENDIX 33:
INDIVIDUAL NDR FILE REQUEST FORM

Individual's Request for National Driver Register (NDR) File Check in Accordance with the Federal Privacy Act of 1974 (Public Law 93-579)

The National Driver Register (NDR) contains only a listing of names and related identification, provided by State driver licensing officials, of those drivers whose driver licenses have been cancelled, denied, revoked, or suspended or who have been convicted of certain serious traffic violations. The NDR does not contain a list of any other drivers. If you have not had a driver license cancelled, denied, revoked, or suspended or have not been convicted of serious traffic violations, you would not be listed in the NDR. Every individual is entitled, however, to request a check of the NDR records to determine whether they appear on the NDR file. The NDR will respond to every valid NDR inquiry.

The record content for those persons who are listed in the NDR files is limited to identification of the state(s) which have taken action to cancel, deny, revoke, or suspend or have records of conviction of serious traffic violations. Any specific information about the driver history, or the entire driver history, may be obtained only from the state(s) where the detailed information is recorded. The state(s) maintaining records are the (only) contacts able to correct records in error, and the NDR will correct its pointer records when so advised by a state indicating that a report previously made to the NDR is in error.

If the NDR has a record on you, the full record will be copied and sent to you including any older records which may have contained a reason for license cancellation, denial, revocation, or suspension. In addition, if such information has been disclosed by the NDR, the recipient of the information will also be identified.

The name and address of the State driver licensing official will be provided for each State listed as having reported information on you to the NDR.

Type or Print Plainly (Avoid delays. Inquiries that cannot be read will not be processed.)

Full Legal Name (First, Middle, and Last)	
Other Names Used (Maiden, Prior Name, Nickname, Professional Name, Other)	
Mailing Address: Number and Street with Apartment or Rural Route/Carrier & Box #	Home Telephone (Optional) Area Code Number ( )
City, State and Zip Code	Work Telephone (Optional) Area Code Number ( )
Driver License Number and State	Soc. Security Number (Optional)
Month, Day, and Year of Birth	Sex / Color of Eyes / Height / Weight
Driver's Signature	Date

NOTARIZATION

Sworn to and ascribed before me

this _____ day of _____

19_____ in the city/county of

_____

State of _____

Form NDR-PRV

Notary Public
Stamp or Seal
(Mandatory)

How to Request an NDR Record Check

Any person may ask to know whether there is an NDR record on him or her and may obtain a copy of the record if one exists. That is the purpose for this form NDR-PRV. Complete the form, have your signature (or your mark as witnessed) notarized, and mail the completed form to the National Driver Register at: 400 7th Street, SW., Room 6124A (NPO-124), Washington, DC 20590-0001. The NDR response will be mailed to the mailing address shown, but incomplete or illegible inquiries will not be processed. All inquiries will be acknowledged if a return address is readable. Forms that are not notarized will not be processed.

What to Expect from the NDR Record Check

The NDR will respond to every valid inquiry including requests that produce no record(s) on the NDR file. When records are located, details of the probable identification results will be returned to you and will contain all information listed in the NDR records, if any, on you. The reply will also indicate any disclosures (reports to others) previously made by the NDR and will specify whom, if anyone has received reports on you.

APPENDIX 34:
EMPLOYEE NDR FILE REQUEST FORM

Request for National Driver Register File Check on Current or Prospective Employee

Current or Prospective Employer to Receive the NDR Search Results: * Driver Employer   * Railroad Company
Employer or Agency Name
To the specific attention of:	Business Telephone Area Code Number ( )
Mailing Address (Number and Street)
City, State and Zip Code

Type or Print Plainly (Avoid delays. Inquiries that cannot be read will not be processed.)

Driver's Full Legal Name (First, Middle, and Last)	
Other Names Used (Maiden, Prior Name, Nickname, Professional Name, Other)	
Mailing Address (Number and Street with Apartment Number if any or Rural Route/Carrier and Box Number)	Home Telephone (Optional) Area Code Number ( )
City, State and Zip Code	Work Telephone (Optional) Area Code Number ( )
Driver License Number and State (Driver must be licensed in the state initiating the search)	Social Security Number (Optional)

Month, Day, and Year of Birth	Sex	Color of Eyes	Height	Weight

EMPLOYEE UNDERSTANDING: I understand that the National Driver Register (NDR) search will result in a printed report which will be sent only to the employer or regulatory agency listed above on this form. The report will indicate either (1) that the NDR does not contain a record matching my identification or (2) that the NDR has a probable identification (match) from one state (or more) which will be named on the report. A separate check of state files would be required (1) to verify the identification or (2) to obtain the driving record. It is the responsibility of the listed employer to obtain the state driver records and to determine or verify records which apply to me. Under the Privacy Act, I have the right to request record(s) pertaining to me from the NDR. I also understand that if convictions, suspensions or revocations of mine are found which I have not shown on my applications or interviews, I might not be hired as a driver or could lose my job as a driver, and the State where I am licensed may also take action on my driver license including suspension, cancellation, or revocation. I hereby, with my signature, authorize a one-time file search of the NDR and any resulting reports to be sent to the employer or agency named on this form.

Driver's Signature (Please read information on back before signing.)	Date

Official Use Only			**NOTARIZATION** Required only if the NDR File Check Request is not made in person by the current or prospective operator.
Date Received	Date Sent	Internal Control	Sworn to and ascribed before me Notary Public Seal or Stamp
			this _____ day of _____
			19_____ in the city/county of
			State of _____
TYPE OF IDENTIFICATION: * Valid Photo Driver License * State-issued Photo ID * Birth Certificate * Valid Passport * Valid Military ID * Military Discharge Papers * Other (specify)			
Employee Verifying Applicant Identification (Print Name) Signature			

Form NDR-EMP

See Reverse Side for Additional Explanations

Requests for National Driver Register (NDR) Record Checks

WHO MAY OBTAIN AN NDR RECORD CHECK

Any person may ask to know whether there is an NDR record on him or her and may obtain a copy of the record if one exists. Requests from individuals require Form NDR-PRV.

Employers of drivers and locomotive engineers may also obtain NDR record checks. *Every driver or operator on whom an NDR file check is requested is entitled to review the NDR report(s) provided to the employer.* The results of the NDR check will be mailed only to the current or prospective employer. If no employer is named on the form or it is changed, the request will not be processed.

The following authorization applies to Railroad Company Requests

NDR CHECK AUTHORIZATION: The U. S. Department of Transportation, Federal Railroad Administration, in accordance with 49 CFR, Part 240.111, requires that I hereby request and authorize the National Highway Traffic Safety Administration (NHTSA) to perform an NDR check of my driving record for a 36-month period prior to the date of this request **including license withdrawal actions open at time of file check.** I hereby authorize the NDR to furnish a copy of the results of this NDR check directly to the railroad company identified on this inquiry form.

WHAT NDR RECORDS CONTAIN

NDR results for employers will contain only the identification of the state(s) which have reported information on the driver to the NDR and only information reported within the past 3 years from the date of the inquiry. Driver control actions initiated prior to that time, even if still in effect, will not be included.

Detailed information to confirm identity or to describe the contents of the driver record can be obtained only from the State(s) listed when probable matches are reported. The name and address of the driver licensing official will be provided for each state listed.

HOW TO REQUEST AN NDR RECORD CHECK

Using this form, which may be completed by either the current or prospective employer or the current or prospective employee, (1) the driver must authorize the request by his or her signature or mark as witnessed and (2) the driver must certify his or her identity. Any mailed NDR record check request must be notarized to certify identity.

Requests must be made to the state in which the driver is licensed.

APPENDIX 35:
DIRECTORY OF STATE NATIONAL DRIVER REGISTRY CONTACTS

STATE	ADDRESS	TELEPHONE
ALABAMA	Department of Public Safety Driver License Records Unit P.O. Box 1471 Montgomery, AL 36192-2301	(334) 242-4142
ALASKA	Department of Administration Division of Motor Vehicles Juneau Driver Licensing 2760B Sherwood Lane Juneau, AK 99801-8545	(907) 465-4363
ARIZONA	Motor Vehicle Division P.O. Box 2100 Driver Improvement Phoenix, AZ 85001	(602) 255-0072
ARKANSAS	Office of Driver Services Driver Control Section P.O. Box 1272 Little Rock, AR 72203	(501) 682-1400
CALIFORNIA	Department of Motor Vehicles Driver License Operations P.O. Box 942890 Sacramento, CA 94290-0001	(916) 657-6525
COLORADO	Motor Vehicle Division Driver Control Section 140 West 6th Avenue Denver, CO 80204	(303) 205-5613
CONNECTICUT	Department of Motor Vehicles Driver Services Division 60 State Street Wethersfield, CT 06109	(860) 263-5720

STATE	ADDRESS	TELEPHONE
DELAWARE	Division of Motor Vehicles Driver Improvement Section P.O. Box 698 Dover, DE 19903	(302) 739-4497
DISTRICT OF COLUMBIA	Bureau of Motor Vehicle Services Traffic Records and Rehab Branch 301 C Street NW. Washington, DC 20001	(202) 727-6761
FLORIDA	Bureau of Records P.O. Box 5775 Tallahassee, FL 32314-5775	(850) 487-4303
GEORGIA	Department of Public Safety Revocation Section P.O. Box 1456 Atlanta, GA 30371	(404) 657-9300
HAWAII	Department of Transportation 869 Punchbowl Street Room 506 Honolulu, HI 96813	(808) 587-6361
IDAHO	Motor Vehicle Bureau Driver Services Section P.O. Box 7129 Boise, ID 83707	(208) 334-8736
ILLINOIS	Department of Motor Vehicles Driver Services Division 2701 South Dirksen Parkway Springfield, IL 62723	(217) 785-3108
INDIANA	Bureau of Motor Vehicles Safety Responsibility Driver Improvement State Office Building Room 410 Indianapolis, IN 46204	(317) 232-2840
IOWA	Driver Records 100 Euclid Park Fair Mall P.O. Box 9204 Des Moines, IA 50306-9204	(515) 237-3086
KANSAS	Division of Vehicles Driver Control Licensing Bureau Robert Docking State Office Building Topeka, KS 66626	(785) 296-3671

STATE	ADDRESS	TELEPHONE
KENTUCKY	Department of Vehicle Regulation Division of Driver Licensing State Office Building, 2nd Floor Frankfort, KY 40622	(502) 564-6800
LOUISIANA	Department of Public Safety Office of Motor Vehicles P.O. Box 64886 Baton Rouge, LA 70896	(225) 925-6009
MAINE	Secretary of State Motor Vehicle Division State House Station 29 Augusta, ME 04333	(207) 624-9000
MARYLAND	Motor Vehicle Administration Division of Driver Records 6601 Ritchie Highway, NE. Glen Burnie, MD 21062	(410) 768-7659,
MASSACHUSETTS	Registry of Motor Vehicles Attn: Suspensions 1135 Tremont Street Boston, MA 02120	(617) 351-7200
MICHIGAN	Department of State Bureau of Driver and Vehicle Records 7064 Crowner Drive Lansing, MI 48918	(517) 322-1460
MINNESOTA	Department of Public Safety 445 Minnesota Street St. Paul, MN 55101-5180	(651) 296-2025
MISSISSIPPI	Department of Public Safety Bureau of Driver Services P.O. Box 958 Jackson, MS 39205	(601) 987-1203
MISSOURI	Drivers License Bureau P.O. Box 200 Jefferson City, MO 65105	(573) 751-2730
MONTANA	Motor Vehicle Division Driver Services Bureau Driver Licensing Records Section 303 N. Roberts Street Helena, MT 59620	(406) 444-4590
NEBRASKA	Department of Motor Vehicles Driver Records Section P.O. Box 94789 Lincoln, NE 68509	(402) 471-3985

STATE	ADDRESS	TELEPHONE
NEVADA	Department of Motor Vehicles Records Services Section 555 Wright Way Carson City, NV 89711-0300	(775) 684-4368
NEW HAMPSHIRE	Division of Motor Vehicles Records Section James H. Hayes Safety Building Hazen Drive Concord, NH 03305	(603) 271-3109
NEW JERSEY	Division of Motor Vehicles Driver Record Abstract Section P.O. Box 142 225 East State Street Trenton, NJ 08666	(609) 292-6500
NEW MEXICO	Division of Motor Vehicles Driver Services Bureau P.O. Box 1028 Santa Fe, NM 87504-1028	(1-888) 683-4636
NEW YORK	Department of Motor Vehicles Driver Licensing Division Swan Street Building Room 221 Empire State Plaza Albany, NY 12228	(518) 474-0735
NORTH CAROLINA	Division of Motor Vehicles Driver License Division 1100 New Bern Avenue Raleigh, NC 27697	(919) 715-7000
NORTH DAKOTA	State Highway Department Driver License Traffic Safety Division 600 E. Boulevard Avenue Bismarck, ND 58505	(701) 328-2603
OHIO	Bureau of Motor Vehicles Driver License Division P.O. Box 16520 Columbus, OH 43266-0020	(614) 752-7500,
OKLAHOMA	Department of Public Safety Driver Improvement Bureau P.O. Box 11415 Oklahoma City, OK 73136	(405) 425-2098
OREGON	Motor Vehicles Division Driver Licensing Section 1905 Lana Avenue NE. Salem, OR 97314	(503) 945-5400

STATE	ADDRESS	TELEPHONE
PENNSYLVANIA	Bureau of Driver Licensing Information Sales Unit P.O. Box 8691 Harrisburg, PA 17105	(717) 787-7154
RHODE ISLAND	Registry of Motor Vehicles Operator Control Section 286 Main Street Pawtucket, RI 02860	(401) 721-2650
SOUTH CAROLINA	South Carolina Department of Public Safety Driver Records P.O. Box 100178 Columbia, SC 29202-3178	(800) 442-1368
SOUTH DAKOTA	Department of Commerce & Regulation Driver Improvement Program 118 W. Capitol Avenue Peirre, SD 57501-2036	(605) 773-6883
TENNESSEE	Department of Safety Driver Control Division 1150 Foster Avenue Nashville, TN 37210	(615) 251-5166
TEXAS	Department of Public Safety Driver Improvement and Control P.O. Box 4087 Austin, TX 78773	(512) 424-2600
UTAH	Motor Vehicle Division Motor Vehicle Records Department P.O. Box 30560 Salt Lake City, UT 84130-0560	(801) 965-3872
VERMONT	Department of Motor Vehicles Driver Improvement 120 State Street Montpelier, VT 05603	(802) 828-2155
VIRGINIA	Department of Motor Vehicles Driver Licensing Info Division P.O. Box 27412 Richmond, VA 23269	(804) 367-0538
WASHINGTON	Department of Licensing Division of Driver Services P.O. Box 9030 Olympia, WA 98504	(360) 902-3900

STATE	ADDRESS	TELEPHONE
WEST VIRGINIA	Department of Motor Vehicles Driver Improvement Division 1800 Washington Street East Charleston, WV 25317	(304) 558-2413
WISCONSIN	Department of Transportation Compliance and Restoration Section P.O. Box 7917 Madison, WI 53707	(608) 266-2261
WYOMING	Department of Transportation Driver Control Financial Responsibility Section P.O. Box 1708 Cheyenne, WY 82003	(307) 777-4800

Source: National Highway Transportation Safety Administration.

APPENDIX 36:
STATE OPEN CONTAINER LAWS

STATE	OPEN CONTAINER LAW
Alaska	driver
Arizona	driver/passenger
Arkansas	n/a
California	driver/passenger
Colorado	n/a
Connecticut	n/a
Delaware	n/a
District of Columbia	driver/passenger
Florida	driver/passenger
Georgia	driver/passenger
Hawaii	driver/passenger
Idaho	driver/passenger
Illinois	driver/passenger
Indiana	driver (only applies if driver has BAC level of 0.04)
Iowa	driver/passenger
Kansas	driver
Kentucky	driver/passenger
Louisiana	driver/passenger
Maine	driver/passenger
Maryland	driver/passenger
Massachusetts	driver/passenger
Michigan	driver/passenger
Minnesota	driver/passenger
Mississippi	n/a

STATE	OPEN CONTAINER LAW
Missouri	n/a
Montana	driver/passenger
Nebraska	driver/passenger
Nevada	driver/passenger
New Hampshire	driver/passenger
New Jersey	driver/passenger
New Mexico	driver/passenger
New York	driver/passenger
North Carolina	driver/passenger
North Dakota	driver/passenger
Ohio	driver/passenger
Oklahoma	driver
Oregon	driver/passenger
Pennsylvania	driver/passenger
Rhode Island	driver
South Carolina	driver/passenger
South Dakota	driver/passenger
Tennessee	driver
Texas	driver/passenger
Utah	driver/passenger
Vermont	driver/passenger
Virginia	n/a
Washington	driver/passenger
West Virginia	n/a
Wisconsin	driver/passenger
Wyoming	driver

Source: Insurance Institute for Highway Safety

GLOSSARY

Adjudicatory Hearing—The process by which it is determined whether the allegations in a complaint can be proven, and, if so, whether they fall within the jurisdictional categories of the juvenile court.

Actively Involved Persons—Includes all drivers or nonoccupants involved in a fatal crash whose actions and characteristics are significant determinants of the crash.

Administrative License Revocation—A law which gives state officials the authority to suspend administratively the license of any driver who fails, or refuses to take, a BAC test.

Alcohol Per Se Laws—Laws which make it illegal to drive with an alcohol concentration measured at or above a certain level.

Alcohol Related Crashes—A crash in which any one of the actively involved persons in a police-reported fatal traffic crash had a BAC of 0.01 or greater.

Alcohol Related Fatalities—A fatality that occurs in a crash where any one of the actively involved persons in the crash had a BAC of 0.01 or greater.

Appearance—To come into court, personally or through an attorney, after being summoned.

Arraign—In a criminal proceeding, to accuse one of committing a wrong.

Arraignment—The initial step in the criminal process when the defendant is formally charged with the wrongful conduct.

Arrest—To deprive a person of his liberty by legal authority.

Bail—Security, usually in the form of money, which is given to insure the future attendance of the defendant at all stages of a criminal proceeding.

Bail Bond—A document which secures the release of a person in custody, which is procured by security which is subject to forfeiture if the individual fails to appear.

Bench Warrant—An order of the court empowering the police or other legal authority to seize a person.

Binge Drinker—Youth admits having 5 or more drinks on the same occasion at last once in the 30 days prior to a survey.

Blood Alcohol Concentration (BAC)—The amount of alcohol in the bloodstream, measured in percentages.

Burden of Proof—The duty of a party to substantiate an allegation or issue to convince the trier of fact as to the truth of their claim.

Capacity—Capacity is the legal qualification concerning the ability of one to understand the nature and effects of one's acts.

CDC—Centers for Disease Control and Prevention.

Commercial Driver License (CDL)—A license issued to an individual which authorizes that individual to drive a class of commercial motor vehicles.

Commissioner—Refers to the Commissioner of motor vehicles of a particular State.

Confession—In criminal law, an admission of guilt or other incriminating statement made by the accused.

Controlled Substance—All substances defined as illegal under the laws of the state, including any other drug or combination of other drugs to a degree which renders a person incapable of safely driving.

Conviction—An adjudication of guilt.

Court—The branch of government responsible for the resolution of disputes arising under the laws of the government.

Craving—As it relates to alcohol, craving is a strong need, or urge, to drink alcohol.

Criminal Court—The court designed to hear prosecutions under the criminal laws.

CSAP—Center for Substance Abuse Prevention, a component of SAMHSA, an operating division within the Department of Health and Human Services.

CSAT—Center for Substance Abuse Treatment, a component of SAMHSA, an operating division within the Department of Health and Human Services.

Culpable—Referring to conduct, it is that which is deserving of moral blame.

Current Drinker—Youth admits having at least one drink in the 30 days prior to a survey.

Damages—In general, damages refers to monetary compensation which the law awards to one who has been injured by the actions of another, such as in the case of tortious conduct or breach of contractual obligations.

D.A.R.E.—Drug Abuse Resistance Education.

DEA—Drug Enforcement Administration, part of the Department of Justice.

Deductible—An amount an insured person must pay before they are entitled to recover money from the insurer, in connection with a loss or expense covered by an insurance policy.

Defendant—In a civil proceeding, the party responding to the complaint.

Defense—Opposition to the truth or validity of the plaintiff's claims.

Delinquent—An infant of not more than a specified age who has violated criminal laws or engages in disobedient, indecent or immoral conduct, and is in need of treatment, rehabilitation, or supervision.

Department—Refers to the department of motor vehicles of a particular State.

District Attorney—An officer of a governmental body with the duty to prosecute those accused of crimes.

Docket—A list of cases on the court's calendar.

DOJ—U.S. Department of Justice.

DOT—U.S. Department of Transportation.

Drive—To drive, operate or be in actual physical control of a vehicle.

Driver—Every person who drives or is in actual physical control of a vehicle.

Driver BAC—The BAC of any driver in in a crash.

Driver's License—Any license to operate a motor vehicle issued under the laws of a particular state.

Drug Episode—An emergency department visit that was related to the use of an illegal drug, or the nonmedical use of a legal drug for patients aged six years and older.

Due Process Rights—All rights which are of such fundamental importance as to require compliance with due process standards of fairness and justice.

Eyewitness—A person who can testify about a matter because of his or her own presence at the time of the event.

Family Purpose Doctrine—The doctrine which holds the owner of a family car liable in tort when it is operated negligently by another member of the family.

Felony—A crime of a graver or more serious nature than those designated as misdemeanors. Under federal law, and many state statutes, any offense punishable by death or imprisonment for a term exceeding one year.

Forfeiture—The loss of goods or chattels, as a punishment for some crime or misdemeanor of the party forfeiting, and as a compensation for the offense and injury committed against the one to whom they are forfeited.

Hallucinogens—Natural and manmade drugs which affect the mind, causing distortions in physical senses and mental reactions.

Hearing—A proceeding during which evidence is taken for the purpose of determining the facts of a dispute and reaching a decision.

Heavy Drinker—Youth admits having 5 or more drinks on the same occasion on at least 5 different days in the month prior to a survey.

Ignition Interlock—A device which has a breath tester that drivers blow into to measure their blood alcohol level and which, if alcohol is detected, prevent the vehicle from starting.

Illegal—Against the law.

Illegal Per Se—Illegal in and of itself.

Impairment—In general, a person is said to be impaired if their BAC level is between 0.01 and 0.07.

Impound—To place property in the custody of an official.

Imprisonment—The confinement of an individual, usually as punishment for a crime.

Jail—Place of confinement where a person in custody of the government awaits trial or serves a sentence after conviction.

Judge—The individual who presides over a court, and whose function it is to determine controversies.

Jury—A group of individuals summoned to decide the facts in issue in a lawsuit.

Jury Trial—A trial during which the evidence is presented to a jury so that they can determine the issues of fact, and render a verdict based upon the law as it applies to their findings of fact.

Juvenile Court—A court which has special jurisdiction, of a parental nature, over delinquent, dependent and neglected children.

Keg Registration Laws—Laws which require beer kegs and other large alcohol containers to be tagged and for the purchasers name and the address where the beverage is to be served to be recorded.

Loss of control—As it relates to alcohol, loss of control means not being able to stop drinking once drinking has begun.

Misdemeanor—Criminal offenses which are less serious than felonies and carry lesser penalties.

Motor Vehicle—Every vehicle which is self-propelled, and every vehicle which is propelled by electric power obtained from overhead trolley wires but not operated upon rails, except vehicles moved solely by human power and motorized wheelchairs.

Narcotics—Generic term for any drug which dulls the senses or induces sleep and which commonly becomes addictive after prolonged use.

NHTSA—National Highway Traffic Safety Administration, part of the Department of Transportation.

No Fault Laws—The insurance laws which provide compensation to any person injured as a result of an automobile accident, regardless of fault.

Nonoccupant—Any person involved in a crash who is not the occupant of a motor vehicle, e.g. Pedestrians and bicyclists.

Nonresident—Every person who is not a resident of the particular State.

Offense—Any misdemeanor or felony violation of the law for which a penalty is prescribed.

Open Container Laws—Laws which prohibit the possession of any open alcoholic beverage container and the consumption of any alcoholic beverage in the passenger area of a motor vehicle.

Owner—A person having the property in or title to a vehicle other than a lienholder.

Pain and Suffering—Refers to damages recoverable against a wrongdoer which include physical or mental suffering.

Pedestrian—Any person on foot.

Peers—Those who are a man's equals in rank and station.

Physical dependence—As it relates to alcohol, physical dependence results in withdrawal symptoms, such as nausea, sweating, shakiness, and anxiety after stopping drinking.

Plea Bargaining—The process of negotiating a disposition of a case to avoid a trial of the matter.

Probable Cause—The standard which must be met in order for there to be a valid search and seizure or arrest. It includes the showing of facts and circumstances reasonably sufficient and credible to permit the police to obtain a warrant.

Prosecution—The process of pursuing a civil lawsuit or a criminal trial.

Prosecutor—The individual who prepares a criminal case against an individual accused of a crime.

Public Defender—A lawyer hired by the government to represent an indigent person accused of a crime.

Recidivism—The tendency to repeatedly relapse into a criminal or delinquent habit such as driving while intoxicated (DWI).

Registration—The registration certificate and registration plates issued under the laws of the State pertaining to the registration of vehicles.

Responsible Beverage Service—Refers to an educational training program that trains and alcohol servers and alcohol outlet managers how to avoid the illegal sale of alcohol to underage youth or intoxicated patrons.

Revocation—The termination by formal action of a person's license or privilege to operate a motor vehicle on the highways, which terminated license or privilege shall not be subject to renewal or restoration except that an application for a new license may be presented and acted upon by the department after the expiration of the applicable period of time.

Search and Seizure—The search by law enforcement officials of a person or place in order to seize evidence to be used in the investigation and prosecution of a crime.

Summons—A mandate requiring the appearance of the defendant in an action under penalty of having judgment entered against him for failure to do so.

Suspension—The temporary withdrawal by formal action of a person's license or privilege to operate a motor vehicle on the public highways, which temporary withdrawal shall be for a period specifically designated.

Tolerance—As it relates to alcohol, tolerance refers to the need to drink greater amounts of alcohol to get "high."

Trial—The judicial procedure whereby disputes are determined based on the presentation of issues of law and fact. Issues of fact are decided by the trier of fact, either the judge or jury, and issues of law are decided by the judge.

Underage Drinking—Underage drinking refers to any child, adolescent, or young person under the age of 21, who drinks alcohol.

Vehicle—Every device in, upon or by which any person or property is or may be transported or drawn upon a highway, excepting devices used exclusively upon stationary rails or tracks.

Verdict—The definitive answer given by the jury to the court concerning the matters of fact committed to the jury for their deliberation and determination.

Warrant—An official order directing that a certain act be undertaken, such as an arrest.

Warrantless Arrest—An arrest carried out without a warrant.

Zero Tolerance Laws—Laws which make it illegal for drivers under age 21 to drive with any measurable amount of alcohol in their system regardless of the BAC limit for older drivers.

BIBLIOGRAPHY AND ADDITIONAL RESOURCES

Al-Anon Family Group Headquarters (Date Visited: May 2004) <http://www.al-anon.alateen.org/>.

Alcoholics Anonymous (Date Visited: May 2004) <http://www.aa.org/>.

Black's Law Dictionary, Fifth Edition. St. Paul, MN: West Publishing Company, 1979.

Campbell, James F, Fisher, P. David and Mansfield, David A.*Defense of Drunk Driving Cases*. New York, NY: Matthew Bender, 3d Edition, 1970 (Supp. 1999).

Centers for Disease Control and Prevention (Date Visited: May 2004) <http://www.cdc.gov/>.

Higher Education Center For Alcohol and Drug Prevention (Date Visited: May 2004) <http://www.edc.org/hec/>.

Insurance Institute for Highway Safety. (Date Visited: May 2004) <http://www.hwysafety.org/>.

Mothers Against Drunk Driving (M.A.D.D.). (Date Visited: May 2004) <http://www.madd.org/>.

Narcotics Anonymous (Date Visited: May 2004) <http://www.nanj.org/>.

The National Center on Addiction and Substance Abuse at Columbia University (CASA) (Date Visited: May 2004) <http://www.casacolumbia.org/>.

The National Clearinghouse for Alcohol and Drug Information (NCADI) (Date Visited: May 2004) <http://www.health.org/>.

The National Commission Against Drunk Driving (NCADD) (Date Visited: May 2004) <http://www.ncadd.com/>.

The National Counsel on Alcoholism and Drug Dependence (NCADD) (Date Visited: May 2004) <http://www.ncadd.org/>.

The National Highway Traffic and Safety Administration (NHTSA) (Date Visited: May 2004) <http://www.nhtsa.dot.gov/>.

The National Institute on Alcohol Abuse and Alcoholism (NIAAA) (Date Visited: May 2004) <http://www.niaaa.nih.gov/>.

The National Institute on Drug Abuse (NIDA) (Date Visited: May 2004) <http://www.drugabuse.gov/>.

Office of the Assistant Secretary for Public Affairs. (Date Visited: May 2004) <http://www.dot.gov/briefing.htm/>.

Substance Abuse and Mental Health Services Administration (SAMHSA) (Date Visited: May 2004) <http://www.samhsa.gov/>.

The Substance Abuse Treatment Facility Locator (Date Visited: May 2004) <http://www.findtreatment.samhsa.gov/>.

United States Bureau of Transportation Statistics. (Date Visited: May 2004) <http://www.bts.gov/>.

The U.S. Department of Health and Human Services (Date Visited: May 2004) <http://www.os.dhhs.gov/>.

U.S. Department of Justice (Date Visited: May 2004) <http://www.usdoj.gov/>.

U.S. Department of Transportation (Date Visited: May 2004) <http://www.usdot.gov/>.